Hilly Laine to
a Brighton Neighbourhood

by Lavender Jones & Jacqueline Pollard

Contents
Forward 2
History 4
Percy & Wagner Almshouses 6
Hanover Crescent 8
Hanover Street 13
Cobden Road Baths 15
Brighton Home for Female Penitants 18
Churches 24
Phoenix Brewery 30
Public Houses 33
Two World Wars 36
Schools 41
Laundries 49
Street Life 53
Shops 65
Maps 75
List of streets & acknowledgements 79

Opposite: 57a Richmond Street on the corner of Windmill Terrace. Frederick and Ada Hills outside their shop with two of their staff c1914. It was F Hills Family Butchers for over 40 years, but was converted to a house in the 1960s.

Cover: Southover Street c1910. Newhaven Street is on the left showing the Hanover Arms. The Fox Inn is visible just above the Tamplin's Brewery site.

Brighton Books Publishing

Forward

"In 1850, the area lying between Hanover Street . . . and Queen's Park, and between the upper part of Sussex Street and Islingword Road, at present covered with houses, was little else than garden ground, with two windmills upon it near the Park. The Freehold Land Society's Estate, which was comprised within a triangle formed by Elm Grove, Islingword Road & Hampden Road, wholly covered by house property in 1870, was twenty years previously used as gardens." J.G. Bishop, 'A Peep into the Past', Brighton Herald Office, 1880.

This photograph was probably taken north west of Elm Grove, an area of small market gardens. In the centre foreground is Hanover Mill (1813-1887) standing where Bernard and Brading Roads are today. In the valley, far right, is Scabes Castle, Lewes Road viaduct and the bridge crossing Hartington Road. A few houses can be seen in Roundhill Crescent, more still in Richmond Road, with the steep flight of steps - the cat creep - connecting the two roads clearly defined. Passing down Wakefield Road to the wooded area, the isolated large houses, Sylvan Hall, Hill Lodge and Wakefield Lodge can be identified. On the brow of the hill behind Richmond Road stands Roundhill Road (1838-1913). On the extreme left at the top, Terminus Road can be seen climbing above the chalk cutting of the railway station, with below the graceful viaduct crossing London Road. St Martin's church is in the valley. The mass of small houses between Lewes Road and Upper Lewes Road are a blur in the centre.

The chapters of this book - a record rather than a history - reflect the experiences of people who have lived and worked in Hanover, some of them in difficult circumstances. In the past, overcrowding, bad housing and poor sanitation were the lot of most people. Many of them had moved to Hanover from areas of the town where conditions were even worse. A few people have lived in Hanover all their lives and behind some of the modernised facades lies a history of poverty that will shock some readers.

Small red paviours or cobbles sometimes appear through the tarmac - designed to stop horses slipping; half obliterated lettering on the side of workshops, a fascia board and shop window on what is now a house, a diagonal doorway on a street corner, revealing that it was once a public house; a bigger building, once an institution, towering over a sea of small terrace houses, or a peep over a crumbling flint wall provide evidence of the history of the neighbourhood.

I first knew Hanover twenty five years ago when some of the buildings were in poor condition and lacked modern amenities. The Council made grants available for repairing the houses and providing modern facilities: bathrooms, kitchens and a hot water supply.

Hanover is still a convivial neighbourhood, but is no longer as self-sufficient as it once was; the horizons of its inhabitants are now very much wider than its boundaries.

Lavender Jones

History

The land beneath what is now known as 'Hanover' was once open arable fields and downland, intersected by pathways and bridleways to Lewes and Rottingdean. At the top of the hill was Tenantry Sheep Down, running up from the Level was Hilly Laine and Islingword Laine. The fields, called laines, were divided into furlongs, and subdivided for cultivation into paul pieces, which ran along the hillside to reduce erosion and soil slip. Access paths on furlong boundaries were called leakways.

The streets were gradually built along the old field pattern, shown in the map at the end of the book. These show Hilly Laine; the Fourth Furlong bounded by Albion Hill and Richmond Street; and Islingword Furlong, bounded by Elm Grove and Islingword Road. The turnpike road at the bottom of the hill is the main road from Brighton to Lewes. The main landowners were Thomas and John Friend, Thomas Western (after whom Western Road was named and who also owned Preston Manor), the Duke of Dorset and others whose names are also remembered by streets elsewhere in the town: Sarah Boyce, Richard Tidy, Philip Mighell; and later the Whichelo family in Hanover.

By 1851 the triangular shape of land bounded by what is now Elm Grove, Queen's Park and Islingword Roads was owned by Wisdon and the Trustees of Matthew Ayers Whichelo. Much of Whichelo's land was let as arable land and the rest was market gardens. Wisdon owned much of the land between Albion Hill and Southover Street; this was still cultivated in the traditional manner by tenants who paid an annual tithe. Tamplin owned the land at the bottom of Albion Hill where the brewery was already providing employment for many local people, and where he kept three cows.

The development of Hilly Laine started when the area south of Edward Street, known as Little Laine, was completed. Between 1804 and 1808 some development took place, this included John,

Thomas, Nelson and Carlton Streets. Building was sporadic from 1808 as land became available, and by 1814 half finished streets of artisan houses and workshops were scattered along the lower slopes of Hilly Laine.

Many developers found the land took a year to sell and were anxious to let it meanwhile. The small strips of land, intermingled with housing, were not of interest to farmers, so other uses such as limekilns, stables, paddocks, cowhouses and market gardens appeared. Edward Tilbury owned twenty seven perches of land, which was occupied by Obidiah Dray in 1851, and this was later to become Chate's Farm. Dray had a cowstall, stable, yard and eight cows for which a tithe of £1.12s was paid.

The main streets which led up the hill were soon occupied by large numbers of shops, public houses, beerhouses and small industries - such as laundries, and soon there was everything the local community needed. The early census shows the diverse occupations of people in the area, many of whom were immigrants from outside the county and from abroad.

Below: the Central Valley from the south-east, a panorama of Brighton extending to its northern limit. The photographer was standing about half way up Richmond Street, facing west across the valley. The field to the right was part of Chate's Richmond Dairy Farm, and the house, no 34, with its roof facing the photographer, was the home of William Chate, and is still there today. The backs of the houses beyond were in Liverpool Street. St Peter's church, Mocatta's Brighton station (in its original unencumbered state with the long low train shed), the railway works and St Bartholomew's church are all visible. The scaffolding which is visible on two sides of St Bartholomew's shows that when the photograph was taken it was still under construction in 1873/4. The small mission church built in 1866 is on the right.
Note the fields on either side of the viaduct. The left hand side of Preston Road (then Roseneath Terrace) and Argyle and Campbell Roads had been built, and can be seen under the central arch of the viaduct.

Alms Houses for six widows near Brighton. These Alms Houses were erected and endowed at the request of the Late Philadelphia and Dorothy Percy 1795. They were part of the Gothick revival. The watercolour is signed on the back 'Ann Stovell. Oct 1807'

The Percy & Wagner Alms Houses

The Percy and Wagner Alms Houses in Lewes Road were built in two phases: the Percy Alms Houses in 1795, and the Wagner Almshouses in 1859. The 1795 almshouses were erected by Mrs Margaret Marriot in memory of her friends Dorothea and Philadelphia Percy, the daughters of the Duke of Northumberland. The six houses were intended for six poor widows who were members of the Church of England within the parish of Brighton, and in 1902 a Coronation gift of £1 was given to the six widows, but there is no mention of the same for the aged maidens.

In addition the women received from Hanningtons shop: two dark brown gowns, not to exceed in value 15 shillings nor less than 12 shillings; and a black bonnet, not exceeding 10 shillings or under 8 shillings and once in three years; a Duffel cloak, which is not to exceed in value 21 shillings nor less than 18 shillings.

The residue of the income was divided amongst the inmates, and paid quarterly. In 1910 this amounted to about 4 shillings per week each.

The remaining six houses were proposed by the Reverend Henry Wagner and his Sister Mary Ann, for six poor maidens. These six were dedicated to the memory of the Marquis of Bristol, who died in 1859.

The 1861 census shows that only the original six houses were occupied:
No. 1   Sarah Rowell. Widow 68 years. Inmate, born Lechlade, Gloucester
No. 1   Ann Kirkham. Unmarried 73 years. Cook, born Henfield, Sussex
No. 2   Phoebe Mullen. Widow 87 years. Laundress, born Kent
No. 2   Martha Bignall. Married 47 years. Laundress, born Pimlico, Middlesex
No. 3   Ann Eynstore. Widow 65 years. Lodging House Keeper, born Lynn, Norfolk
No. 4   Mary Lloyd Head. Widow 76 years. Dealer, born Salisbury, Wilts.
No. 5   Mary Ann Rushton. Widow 65 years. Nurse, born Portsea, Hants.
No. 5   Mary Ann Rushton. Unmarried 45 years, Needlewoman.
No. 5   Alfred Rushton. Grandson ,8 years. Scholar, born Brighton, Sussex
No. 6   Mary ? Widow 63 years. Needlewoman, born Hertford, Hertfordshire.

Percy & Wagner Almshouses c1970

It is surprising that some of these small houses were occupied by more than one person, and it is apparent that family members were able to live with the original occupant. Most of the women give an occupation rather than 'Inmate of Almshouse' as their occupation, and none of the women were born in Brighton.

The 1891 census shows all twelve of the Alms Houses occupied, with Prudence Davey, a widow of 69, from Hurst in Sussex, living with her granddaughter Louisa aged eleven at no 4, and Selina Fuller, unmarried aged 63, from Whitting in Sussex, living with her niece Lily Louisa Shelley aged fourteen at no 10. All the other houses had one resident, one with a visitor on census night. Six of the residents were single women and six were widows with only one resident born in Brighton.

When the Reverend Wagner died in 1870, he left £100 to a former servant, Jane Scrase, who was at that time resident in the almshouse. This gives an indication of the type of woman who might be resident there, respectable working ladies of no independent means.

The 1901 accounts show that cloaks were purchased from Hannington's and builders were paid for repairs. By 1903 residents were given allowances in lieu of bonnets and later in lieu of cloaks as well. In 1930 there appears to be an item of £95 for the installation of gas and water to the houses. Prior to this, it was candles, coal and a pump in the yard.

By 1971 the almshouses were in a state of disrepair, only one was occupied and the others unfit for habitation. The Trustees wanted to demolish them, but they were listed in 1971 and restoration began five years later. New kitchens and bathrooms were built in extentions at the rear of the houses and the interiors were redesigned, keeping the original facade.

The funds from the charity were insufficient to enable the buildings to be brought up to the required standard, so the Borough Council helped with additional funds, and as a result were able to nominate tenants for nine of the twelve houses.

N.W. VIEW OF HANOVER CRESCENT, BRIGHTON

Hanover Crescent

Brighton had begun to develop northwards towards the Lewes Road by 1822. The working class area of Carlton Hill, with its small tenement houses, abundance of public houses, workshops and slaughterhouses, had been the most northerly development until 1795, when the Percy Almshouses were built in a rural setting at the junction of Lewes Road and Race Hill Road.

It was in the area between Carlton Hill and the almshouses that Henry Brooker decided to build a middle class crescent of houses. Work on the houses started in 1809 and was completed by 1822, with other substantial villas developing along the main road at the same time. In c1814 Henry Brooker employed architects Wilds and Busby to design a facade for the Crescent, with building lots being sold to individuals, enabling the rest of the house to be designed to the purchasers' own requirements.

When complete Hanover Crescent was a semi-circle of twenty four houses with bow fronts, shell motifs and Corinthian and Ammonite pilasters, though they were not of a uniform design. The two lodges at each end of the Crescent were single storey buildings with Tuscan columns and pediments. Gates and iron railings enclosed the Crescent in front of the semi-circular carriage drive. Title deeds describe the erection of gates "to keep our road a private road for the exclusive use and enjoyment of the tenants and occupiers free from horse, cattle carts and other carriages." Tenants were to pay equal amounts for the maintenance and upkeep of grounds.

During the construction of the Crescent Wilds lived at Richmond Lodge, with his builder's yard on the Level opposite his house. Charles Burchett, a builder, at 22 Richmond Buildings, whose private residence was at 1 Southover Street, was involved with the interior design of the Crescent.

In 1821, just as the select development of Hanover Crescent was being completed, the Phoenix Brewery opened on land stretching from Albion Hill to Southover Street. The Level recreational area was laid out opposite the Crescent and construction of the new parish church of St. Peter's was started. The Crescent, a select development for middle class residents, was now in a more socially mixed neighbourhood, and this would have an affect on the type of occupant.

Hanover Crescent initially attracted well known residents such as Horace Smith, the writer and poet, who lived at no 10 from 1826-1840. His house was a meeting place for the intellectual society of Brighton and among his friends were Dickens and Thackery. He was succeeded in this house by Samuel Hood; a physician, and father of the first Viscount British Admiral.

Opposite: 4 Hanover Crescent. George Rush lived here c1905 when the photograph was believed to have been taken

Hanover Crescent in the 60s

In 1851 George Brown, a well known cricketer of the time, lived at no 10. He was the keeper of the Hanover Cricket Ground, now Park Crescent, with its entrance gate in the centre of the flint wall in Union Road. In 1839 Mr Henry James lived at no 11, but by 1844 Roland Hill, the originator of the penny post and the chairman of the London & Brighton Railway Company, lived there. Henry Brooker himself lived at no 14 for about twenty five years, after which the house was purchased by Elizabeth Guiness, a brewer's wife and at one time Lady Mayoress of Dublin.

John George Bishop, writer of local history and editor of the Brighton Herald, lived at no 15, which became the official residence of the Vicar of Brighton from 1839-1882. The Crescent was home to no less than fifteen parsons from 1822-1907. G F Attree Junior, auctioneer and estate agent, lived at no 8 from 1884-1906, the first resident to have a telephone. When the house was sold it was combined with no 9 to make Hanover House, which became St Paul's Convent School run by a Mother Superior from Belgium.

Charles Hammond bought no 18 Hanover Crescent in 1824, but his stay was short lived as he was declared bankrupt and the property sold at auction on the premises on 13 April 1826. The description of the contents gives an insight into the furnishings of that time:

"All the handsome and modern household furniture; consisting of lofty four post bedsteads with carved mahogany pillars, and tastefully arranged chintz and dimity furnitures; large sized and well seasoned goose feathered beds; hair and wool mattresses; Witney blankets and counterpanes; capital mahogany chests of drawers, night commodes, basin stands, dressing, Pembroke, card, dining and claw tables; handsome Brussels carpets; large size chimney, pier and dressing glasses; stuffed horse hair sofa with rich chintz furniture; mahogany and japanned chairs; half-tester bedstead, with neat printed furniture etc; an assortment of plate and linen; a quality of oil cloth and Venetian stair carpeting; together with a general collection of kitchenware."

The house was purchased by William Henry Klyne, a retired Receiver of Taxes!

Opposite: Ordnance Survey map of Hanover Crescent surveyed in 1875

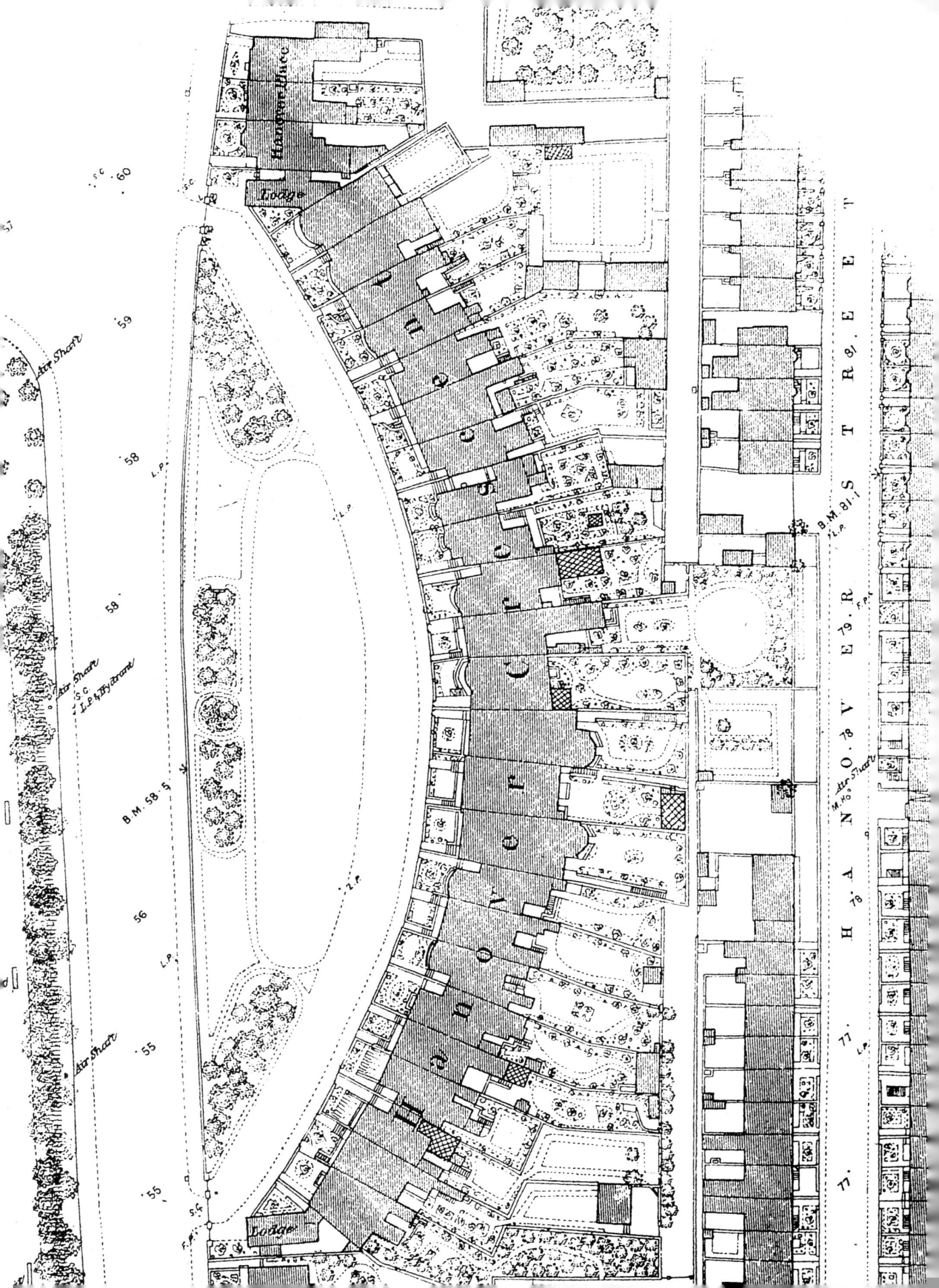

Mr. Smith Hannington of the drapery trade left his house in Hanover Crescent to Mr Samuel Hannington in 1826, later it was ccupied by an accountant of Hanningtons. No 19 was bought by the Brighton Co-operative Society in 1929, which they extended at the rear to form a dairy, supplying milk to the area until quite recently.

Of the 24 houses in Hanover Crescent on census night, 30 March 1851, 23 were occupied and one was empty. One property had only a maid in residence and therefore only 22 households had a head of household. Of the 22 heads of household 10 were married men, 3 widowers, 2 widows, 6 single females and 1 married female. No females were marked on the census as having an occupation other than fundholders, annuitants and a retired governess. Some of the residents of Hanover Crescent appear in the Court Directory, indicating a certain wealth and standing. Of the 22 heads of household none were born in Sussex. Most of the heads of household were retired or fundholders so they did not have to earn a living and were therefore able to live on the edge of the town. Each family had at least two servants and possibly had other staff who lived out, as several women in nearby Hanover Street and Hanover Terrace state their profession as housemaids.

Hanover Cresent: a drawing by Walter de la Mare, 1853

Damaged lettering on the house on the corner of Hanover and Southover Streets

Hanover Street

Henry Brooker, the original developer of Hanover Crescent, also commissioned a small street of houses to be built directly behind the Crescent, to be called Hanover Street.

The Brighton Gazette, 20 June 1822 carried the following advertisement:

"To be Let - on building leases with purchasing clauses. A very Eligible Freehold Ground at the back of Hanover Crescent. Intended to form a street, and houses to be set back 14' on each side of the street, to form forecourts or garden plots for each tenement, so that the distance between the houses will be 58'. Roads about 10' wide at each end of the street are intended to be made from the Lewes Road to Hanover Street. For particulars apply to Mr Penfold Solicitor, Princes Place or to Mr A H Wilds, Builder, Level, Brighton."

A map c1822 shows the planned Hanover Street running behind the Crescent before construction had started, but in Baxter's Strangers' Guide of 1824, Hanover Street is listed as small tenements. The houses were small, some two, some three storeys, built piecemeal with no uniform design, large pieces of land remaining undeveloped for years.

Indentures relating to nos 73-74 Hanover Street show that a Mr William Penfold the younger, living at 71 Middle Street, purchased a piece of land to the west of Hanover Street which he left to his wife Mary on his death in 1868. In 1873 Mary Penfold left the house to John Croucher Penfold, a solicitor, who sold the property to Walter Boniface for £115 in 1877. Mr. Boniface lent £150 to Mr Albert Henry Wilson, coal merchant, so that he could purchase the property from him. By May 1878 Mr Wilson had paid back the loan and owned the property, which, with the house and land next to it, were used for his coal business.

In the 1881 census Albert Wilson, aged 35, and his wife Martha, aged 38, shared nos 73 & 74 with their four children and a servant aged 14. By 1891 Albert Wilson, a coal merchant from Midhurst, still lived at no 73 with his wife Martha, a daughter Florence and a cousin who was a servant, with no 74 used as a coal shed. Arthur, son of Albert Wilson, sold the property in 1914 to Mr William Thomas Bradshaw, Auctioneer's Clerk, for £230, £100 of this being repaid to Mrs. Anna Alice Bates, widow, who had loaned Mr Wilson money. Later that year Mr. Bradshaw sold the property to Miss Albertina Maud Mathias for £250, whom he married a month later. An astute move on his behalf!

The property continued to be used as a coal merchant's from time to time until the 1930s. Mrs. Bradshaw gave the house to Mr Thomas Alfred Tillman in a deed of gift in 1957. He had been the chauffeur to William Bradshaw and was also head projectionist at the Duke of York's cinema. He lived there with his large family of twelve children, cooking on a range set into a chimney breast and bathing in a tin bath in front of the fire. Leslie Wilson, his son, took over joint ownership with his wife in 1988 and sold the property to the present owner in 1991, the first time the house had been sold for 77 years.

Hanover Street had forty five dwellings registered on census night in 1851, which included sixty eight heads of household. Some of the houses had two or three different families living in them, possibly one on each floor. The census shows that the majority of the heads of household in Hanover Street were from Sussex, probably attracted to the town with the prospect of obtaining work. Most were unskilled and had possibly previously worked on farms. Unlike the heads of household in Hanover Crescent, few came from the London area, but sixteen out of sixty eight came from counties further away. The occupants of Hanover Street included: nineteen labourers, nine carpenters, five gardeners and five grooms/carriage drivers, an invalid chairman, a retired sailor and a Chelsea pensioner. Of the heads of households eleven were women, nine of whom were laundresses, one needlewoman and one English teacher. Of the nine laundresses, seven were widows, one married and one single. Much of the open land above Hanover Crescent was used as drying fields for laundries. In all there were twenty women in Hanover Street involved in laundry work including three ironers. The women in Hanover Street, especially those without a husband to support them, would have had a hard life relying on hand washing for their income.

In 1864, an observer remembered what the area used to be like:

"There were only a few houses scattered here and there, among market gardens, made on the side of what once formed part of the Brighton Downs. Now there are sixteen streets of small, modern houses for artisans; eight streets in parallel lines, intersected by the upward road. Two streets are occupied by small shopkeepers of various trades. At one pm the streets are thronged by men returning from the station works for their dinner; this shows the occupation of many of the inhabitants. Others were employed in various houses of business, or do shop work at home. There are also a great number of small laundries: with the exception of the bottom row of houses facing the main road [Hanover Crescent] which are of a somewhat superior kind, the whole parish is essentially poor."

'The Hollow'

A twitten runs between Hanover Street and Hanover Terrace and is known locally as 'The Hollow'. There used to be a public house 'The Little Fox', on one corner and a shop on the other, the overhanging fascia boards are evidence of their former use.

In 1976 it was threatened with a stopping up order by Brighton Council, as they had received a petition from eighty three local residents calling for its closure as it was being misused by local children. Two days before the Highways and Transport Committee of the Council applied to the court for a closure order another group of residents submitted a counter-petition with ninety two signatures. Mrs Betty Parker of Hanover Terrace said, "[the twitten] was a great help to the elderly and disabled and one of them was nearly in tears when she thought it would be closed." Robert Gregory of the Brighton Society said that "the 156 year old twitten was of historic interest and should be preserved." It remains open to this day.

The public house, The Little Fox, the entrance to The Hollow at 22 Southover Street and a shop

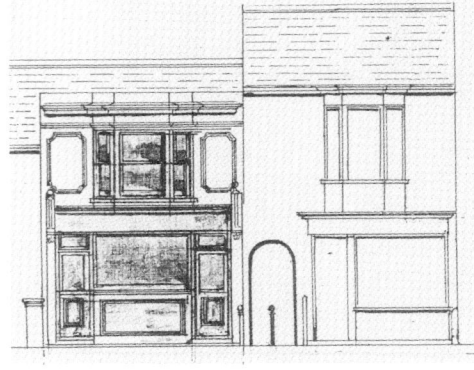

Cobden Road Public Baths

Cobden Road public slipper baths were opened in April 1894 by Sir Joseph Ewart, the Mayor, after whom Ewart Street was named. A red brick building with shell and dolphin decorations at the corners, it soon became a popular facility in the area.

When Hanover was designated an Improvement Area in the 1970s, bathrooms were installed in many of the houses for the first time and demand for the public baths dropped. The Cobden Road Baths were closed in 1976 and the building was used as the Hanover Community Centre until 1982, then as a resource centre until its conversion into flats in 1985-6. The conversion did not alter the facade and the inaugural tablet still remains in the entrance hall.

I lived in Islingword Road in the 20s and 30s and used Cobden Road Baths. Mr and Mrs Gillam and their daughter Eileen ran the baths at the time. I went every week, it was two pence for a bath, three pence with a towel.

Mr G Hayward

On Saturdays I would meet up with friends and go to the wonderful Cobden Road Baths. The water was deep and we would call out "More hot in number five please," in order to keep the water temperature up.

Susan Davies

My mother worked at Cobden Road Baths for a while, but it was being repainted and they refused to close it whilst the work was being done. She developed painters' colic and had to leave.

Mrs E Campbell nee Boyett

My father worked for the Brighton Council Waterworks division and was therefore involved with Cobden Road Baths and looked after the big piece of ground between the reservoir wall and the back of the old soup kitchen. The building fronting Cobden Road was a very old one storey Victorian Building which always looked very ramshackle and had a funny smell to it. The Baths were sold by Brighton Corporation in the 1980s and Southern Water now control the waterworks so it has all changed. The old cottage was demolished in the 1950s and nothing has been built on the site since.

Mr Walter Hope

Entrance and exit to the soup kitchen. Overleaf: floor plans and facade of Cobden Road Baths

Ground and first floor plans

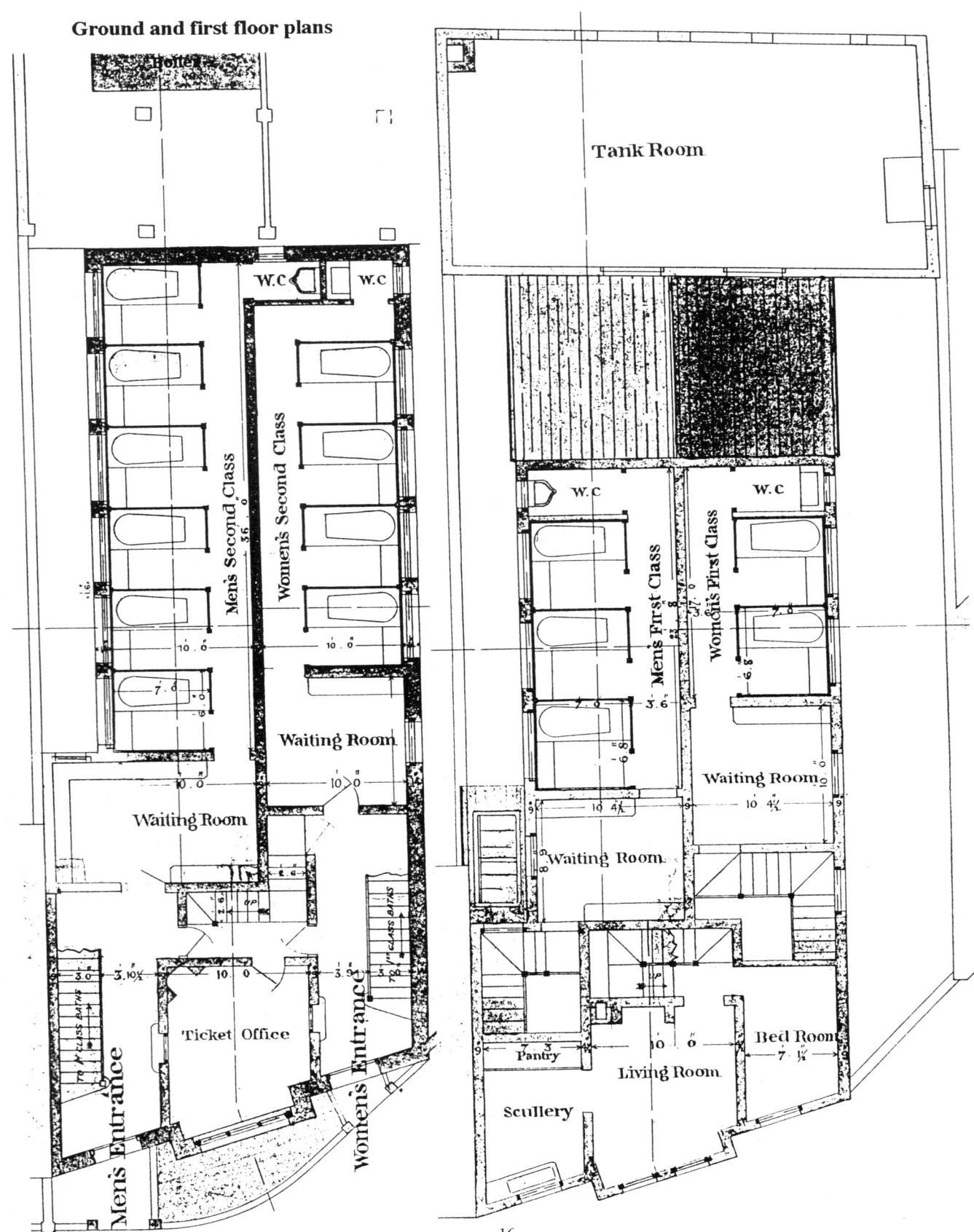

The building was erected in 1870 at the expense of the Reverend George Wagner and was known as the Brighton Home for Penitent Females. It provided a refuge for unmarried mothers who worked in the laundry attached to the Home. In 1918 it was closed as a result of lack of funds, but was opened the following year as the Albion Church Army Home for Girls. By 1947 it reverted partly to its original purpose, known then as the Church Army Maternity and Child Welfare Home. It was demolished in 1958, the year this photograph was taken.

Brighton Home for Penitent Females

People's Magazine, 1 July 1899 - 'Work Among the Lost' by the author of 'Home Thoughts for Working Women and Mothers' Meetings.'

"George Wagner, who having been ordained had taken the district church of St Stephen's Brighton [on the corner of Canning Street and Sutherland Road], was walking down one of the back streets of that place, when three girls, with no bonnets on their heads, passed in front of him, talking in loud coarse tones, and laughing wildly with 'that laughter that is not mirth.' At once he felt that they were outcasts from God and men, yet with immortal souls, capable of being redeemed, capable of 'shining as the stars for ever and ever'. At once a forgotten sermon rushed into his mind - the sense that he was responsible for them and for thousands like them if he made no effort to save them; and in a moment the buried seed of ten years sprang to life.

. . . George Wagner and Mrs Vicars worked for three months, . . . rescued thirty girls and took them to London to various refuges, but when the London refuges couldn't take any more it became necessary that a home should be provided in Brighton. An appeal was made and quickly responded to, . . . a small house opposite the Level was taken and fifteen penitents were also lodged in a larger house on the Lewes Road.

[The] building which stands on one of the hills immediately behind Brighton, [is] known by the name of the Albion Hill Home for Female Penitents. A pretty building, it is bright and pleasant to look at, set round with its glossy evergreens, and overlooking the valley below, spanned by its noble viaduct, and the distant hills breathing in their blue tranquillity

. . . The building itself is bright and pleasant to the eye, and as you enter, you are shown into large bright airy rooms, the walls are hung with bright pictures, and pretty illuminated texts; floods of sunshine stream in at the large windows; no vexatious inflictions, such as cutting the hair short, are in force; the common dress of the institution differs little from that of an ordinary servant; and remembering that the inmates come fresh from the wild license of an uncontrolled life, the monotony of the day's work is broken by being turned out for an hour's good play in the garden in summer, with swings, skipping ropes, gardening, and all kinds of games in full force; while in winter they are supplied with quiet indoor games and amusements. They are not encouraged to make much profession of religion while in the Home, nor is attendance at many religious services exacted from them.

. . . The daily rules of the Albion Hill Home are that the inmates rise at 5.30 am in summer and 6.30 am in winter, and work until 8 pm, being allowed an hour for dinner, and half an hour for their other meals. . . they are allowed an hour for recreation from 8 pm until 9 pm. Simple instruction is given three times a week, in reading, writing, and summing; but the attendance is more or less optional, though most take advantage of it. On Sunday they go to church in the morning, but in the afternoon a service is held in their own little chapel by the chaplain.

A girl on being admitted is placed at once on the probationers' ward [with] the private laundry, where all the washing of the Home itself is done, so that she learns the whole business of washing, ironing, and getting up, on the clothes belonging to the institution. Thence she passes, a tolerably practised hand, into the public laundry, by which arrangement the Institution is enabled to take in washing for a higher class than can usually be done by inexperienced hands, and to turn out the best laundry work, nearly £1,000 being annually made by washing and needlework combined. The Home also had the idea that using physical strength worked off unhealthy thoughts and the girls enjoyed the face to face contact with the other girls. Having thoroughly learnt the work of the laundry, the girl passes into the kitchen, where she is taught the duties of a kitchen maid; and thence she passes finally into the work-room, where she is trained in needlework and the use of the sewing machine. The girls are carefully taught to feel that the Home is not a prison house - that at any time they demand the old clothes they came in and, persuasion proving useless to induce them to stay, they may take their departure. But those who hope to obtain a situation are expected to remain in training two years . . . at the end of which time a complete outfit of clothes is given to them, a Bible, a Prayer Book, and a writing case, and they are placed in an eligible situation, a gift of ten shillings being given to them if they keep it for a year. This they seldom fail to claim; and thus the way is open before them to a respectable, happy, and useful life."

The 1871 census indicates nine members of staff: a matron and her assistant, a wash house supervisor, a laundry matron and her assistant, a housekeeper and her husband, a carpenter, a probation matron and a monitor; and sixty one inmates: the youngest - Elizabeth Avery - aged 11 from Brighton, and the oldest Charlotte Hayner, a widow aged 41, from Middlesex. Of the sixty one inmates only twenty came from Brighton. There were four pairs of sisters including May and Harriet Yates from Brighton, aged 14 and 13. In 1881 there were fourteen staff and forty eight girls between the ages of 15 and 19, and their occupations were mostly laundry and kitchen maids. One of them was a Mary Waas aged 18, occupation needlewoman, born in Rotterdam, Holland. By 1891 there were eight staff and thirty six inmates many of whom came from other parts of the country. By 1894 there was accommodation for eighty inmates.

During 1911 one hundred and twenty girls were living at the institution; forty having left, thirty two of whom had been sent into service, ten were returned to friends and six left of their own will, of whom three were subsequently re-admitted, leaving seventy two girls on the roll on 31 December. The annual report shows that circumstances, outwardly anyway, may have improved since the seemingly draconian regime of the home in the previous century.

"Gratuities of 10s each were awarded to eight girls who kept their first situation for twelve months. Kind and loving treatment, regular hours for active employment, systematic Bible teaching, moral and useful instruction under the superintendence of the chaplain, Mrs Macdonald, and the efficient matron and her staff, who exercise loving tact, wise and firm control and enduring patience - all these have had the effect of transforming character to such a large degree as to surpass the hopes of the most sanguine."

The character of the education given in the present day was, he thought, another cause. Young people needed the kind of education that was formerly in the good old parochial schools; he felt the want of religious instruction caused many to err.

The Reverend A E Wynne, the then Vicar of Rottingdean, . . . also referred to overcrowding, which he said prevailed not only in towns, but in the country as well. He hoped for much from the Housing and Town Planning Act. A great deal of evil they were fighting against was caused by a certain amount of feeble-mindedness in girls. He praised the work done in Brighton as really great, noble, and useful.

The Coronation of George V on June 23 1911 was cause for celebration and the day was observed as a holiday in the Home. The Committee gave a grant of £5 towards the festivities and after a thanksgiving service in the chapel, each girl was presented with a Coronation Testament, a framed card, and a medal.

There were 'suitable' decorations in and outside the buildings, and in the evening Chinese lanterns and fairy lights added to the festive appearance; which must have illuminated what was normally a rather gloomy Victorian building.

Extract from a letter published as an advertisement for the Home. Letter from Mistresses:

"I have had three or four girls from the Home, and they have turned out good servants and have done well. I have a girl now in my service, I had a little trouble with her at first, but she is now a very steady, good girl, and a capital, hardworking servant."

In 1916, during the First World War, my mother had my eldest sister in the Finsbury Road Home. She was unmarried and the father of the child was in the army. Mother had twelve brothers and sisters but not one of them offered to help her. She stayed at the home for most of her pregnancy and she was very unhappy there. She told me that it was an awful place. The girls slept in dormitories, and during the day had to scrub the stone floors and work in the laundry.

Although she had not received much support from her family in the beginning, her grandmother offered to look after her daughter after she was born, instead of her being sent to an orphanage, as most of the babies were. Her grandmother lived in a small cottage in Patcham Village and for five happy years my sister lived there with her. Unfortunately her grandmother died when my sister was five and she was then fostered for a year until my mother married and was able to look after her herself. My father accepted my sister as his own and my sister idolised him, she could never tell that she was not his child and was shocked when she found out.

Unfortunately the stay in the home caused my mother to suffer from depression and she committed suicide in 1952, the day before my sister's birthday.

Patricia Sprinthall

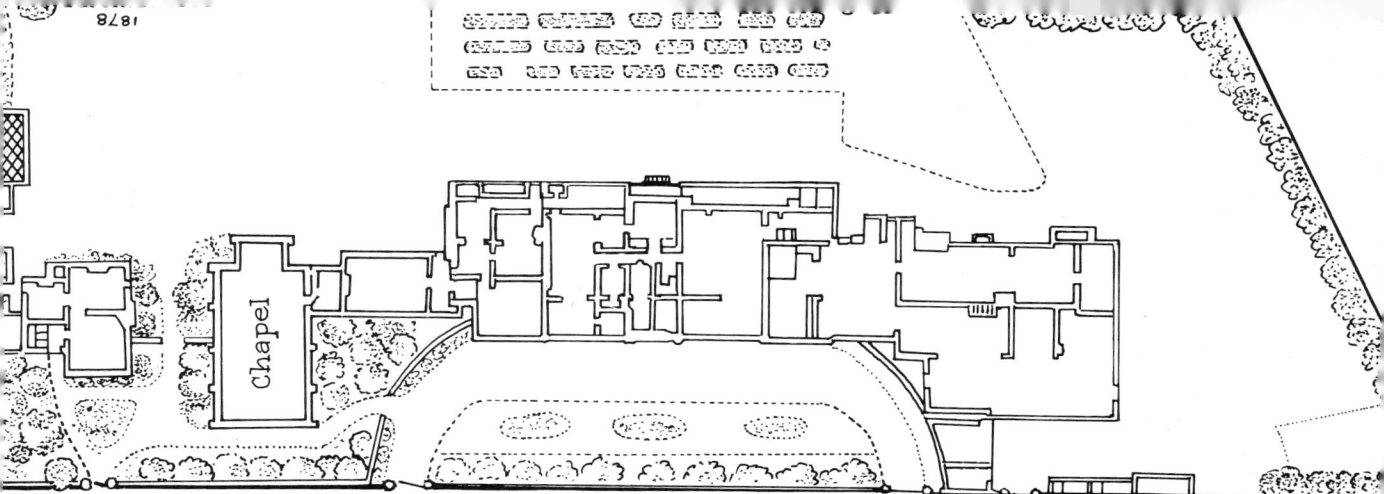

I attended Finsbury Road Infants and Junior school until I was fourteen. Opposite the school was the Church Army Home for unmarried mothers run by several Sisters from the Church Army. Every morning when all the children were at school, the girls were taken out in groups of about twelve for a walk in Queen's Park. They were not pitied, most people thought that they had made their own bed and had to lie on it, but many of the girls had been slung out of home. Most of the babies were adopted. The girls were kept away from the children in the school because they thought that we would 'barrack' them.

Mr G Harwood.

Two ladies in Montreal Road also looked after girls who were pregnant. The girls were paid for privately by their families and the girls would return home after the birth and the babies would be adopted. The ladies adopted two of the children.

Olive Denman, deceased

As a young man I lived in Carlyle Street. I remember the girls from the Church Army Home in Finsbury Road walking in a crocodile. They always had a uniformed official with them as they walked along Tower Road, East Drive, West Drive and back home again. I must have been 10 or 11 and with a group of boys we would cat call 'The Pudding Club's coming'.

A resident

The Church Army Home was a grim building enclosed by a brick and flint wall. The girls were taken out for walks in groups, usually accompanied by a very severe looking woman.

Mrs E Campbell nee Boyett

I lived opposite the Church Army Home for Unmarried Mothers for 30 years and when I was in the Junior School the matron used to let me go over and bath the babies.

Mrs J Fennell

I lived at 18 Southampton Street when I was young, so we saw the girls from the 'bad girls home' walking in a crocodile on their daily outing. Years later I went for an interview for a job at Bevan Funnell who had taken over the building. It seemed a bit grim to me, a typical Victorian home and I didn't fancy working there.

Mrs Janet Webb nee Jenner

The fallen girls who were at Finsbury Road were marched down Elm Grove for their morning stroll. Some of the girls had tried to get rid of the babies by taking a herb remedy called Penny Royal, but without much success.

Mary Bray

I lived at 11 Queen's Park Road in the late 1930s; on Sunday mornings at 9.40 a crocodile of twenty or more girls would walk down the road to morning service at St Mary's Kemp Town, two very stern nuns in the front, and two more at the rear. All the girls had scrubbed, red - perhaps with embarrassment - faces, and clothes stretched tight across their stomachs - no maternity clothes in those days. Upon hearing the marching feet mother would come out and call my sister and me in from the little front courtyard where we were playing saying "Quickly, here come the naughty girls", and in we would go. The same thing happened when they all marched back on the other side of the road. I'm not sure if I realised why they were called 'the naughty girls', but remember thinking how young and poor some of them were.

Mrs June Marshall nee Pearce

'The Story of Bevan Funnell Ltd' by Pamela Bevan Funnell and 'Brighton Ghosts' by Frank Usher.

The harsh poor laws and the unfeeling treatment of unmarried mothers caused untold suffering and unhappiness. Many were probably glad to see the building pulled down, but it remained empty for many years and the council was hard put to find a suitable tenant. A large Gothic building with a floor area of 12,000 sq ft, it was not suitable for many businesses, but in 1952 the building was leased to furniture manufacturer Bevan Funnell Ltd. Machinery was stored in the basement, offices were on the ground floor, a polishing shop on the first floor, and the chapel was used as the despatch department. Forty staff were employed, their ages ranging from 15-50.

Mrs Bevan occupied what had been the matron's office, together with her mother and a part-timer who did filing, etc. Mr Funnell was at that time a member of Hove Borough Council and became Mayor of Hove in 1960. He was also a Special Constable, and both he and his wife were practical, matter-of-fact business people. The Bevan family also had a mongrel dog called Blarney, who accompanied them to the factory every day.

Then strange, unexplained things started to happen. The police warned the Bevans that the doors to the building were found unlocked at night. This was strange, as the caretaker who lived on the premises made sure the building was secure, but even padlocked doors were found to be unlocked. Furniture would be turned over and chairs moved, but little damage could be found.

Then one evening as it was getting dark, a driver was working in the packing room on the first floor. Turning, he saw a woman standing in the doorway dressed in a black suit; as he spoke to her she disappeared. He ran to the door and up the passage, but there was no sign of her; he came down the stairs and related what he had seen, but the others made light of it.

Shortly afterwards Mrs Bevan was working late one night, as she often did, Blarney the dog at her side. She noticed later that he was missing and became aware of him whimpering on the first floor above the office. She went upstairs to see what was wrong and entered the long room which had been divided down the middle many years ago by a sliding partition. The Bevans were using it as a storeroom and had been unable to move the divider as it was rusted solid. As Mrs Bevan opened the door she noticed the divider had been moved across the room without a sound in the office below. The dog was trapped behind the partition. Mrs Bevan ran downstairs calling to the men who were loading a van, who ran back with her and together managed to push the partition enough to get the dog out. It remained immovable after that.

The Funnells and their staff were convinced that the building was haunted. They began to make inquries about its history and discovered it had been a home for unmarried mothers. In Victorian times such institutions were often grim places run on penal lines.

In the centre of the building was a small room the Bevans used as an office. Across the passage was a cloakroom and lavatory. One day in the passage a strong perfume could be smelt by all the staff. Mrs Funnell described it as a musky smell almost like incense, but peculiarly feminine and sensuous. Sometimes this perfume would seem to blow in waves around the building; no one could ever discover its origins. One day a heavily knitted cardigan in black wool appeared mysteriously in the cloakroom. It was hanging on a peg and was deeply impregnated with this strange perfume. No one owned it. and a day or two later it disappeared and was never seen hanging there again. The Funnells suspected they were being subjected to tricks being played upon them by someone wanting them to vacate the building, but even if this was so, some of the things that happened were inexplicable.

The typewriter in the office would often be heard typing furiously when no one was in the room. When the door was opened the noise stopped. As was to be expected, the Funnells had problems with the staff over the haunting. Many were scared off, others laughed at the idea of ghosts and others stuck it out of loyalty to the firm.

In 1953, a year after the Funnells took over the building, some local spiritualists held a seance there. Mrs Funnell attended this seance, during which a girl was supposedly contacted, speaking in a Sussex accent she said "Matron is cruel to me, I am desperately unhappy; I've tried to be good, but I can't." "She sounded a miserable little thing", said Mrs Funnell. The Funnells were sceptical about this seance.

Nevertheless, a strange thing happened immediately after the seance had finished. As soon as the spiritualists had left, there was a tremendous noise of people running all over the building, of doors banging, people calling and of pounding footsteps, followed by silence. This silence lasted until the Sunday before Christmas of 1954, when Mr Funnell went to the office by himself to catch up with a backlog of work. By then the past happenings had been forgotten and he was only concerned with the rush of Christmas orders. It was a bright December day. As he went into the office he heard a thud, as though a book had been dropped, he looked along the built-in bench around the walls, and what he saw haunted him for the rest of his life.

Appearing through one of the benches was a human figure. The bench could be seen through it and it seemed to turn towards Mr Funnell. As it slowly turned he could see what he described as 'a face shape with eyes'. The feeling he had was that someone was looking at him with incredible hatred and loathing, which filled him with overwhelming fear. He fled from the room and out of the building. "I felt waves of hate coming at me and I was utterly terrified," he said as he described later to his wife what he had seen. He returned at lunchtime ashen, his eyes sunken and it was many hours before he recovered himself. Mr Funnell was so shaken by this experience that he decided to obtain the services of a priest to come and exorcise the premises. They found a local man who arranged an exorcism, after which they had no more trouble from hauntings.

A few years later the Funnells left the building and it was immediately demolished by the Council, who quickly built a block of flats on the site. The Funnells heard later that the occupants of the flat which would have been in that part of the building where the supposed hauntings had been, complained to the Council that they were continually having trouble with draughts, windows opening, noises, doors thrown open, books thrown around and so on. So it would seem there may have been more than one troubled spirit, judging by the the uproar sometimes heard.

Churches

The Church of Annunciation

The Church of Annunciation, between Washington Street and Coleman Street, was designed and built by William Dancy in 1864, with additions by Edmund Scott in 1881. The Reverend Arthur Douglas Wagner saw the workers' cottages springing up amongst the market gardens on the hill in the 1850's and was determined to build a church in the area. The fashionable Brighton churches drew crowds and charged pew rents, but this church was to be a place which was free and devoted only to its immediate neighbourhood.

The church was opened on 15 August 1864, The Feast of The Assumption. A school for girls and infants was originally provided below the church, open to the air on three sides. In 1865 plans were lodged for the building of a boys' school in Southover Street, now the Community Centre. Even after the Education Act, several hundred children were still catered for in the Sunday School. It was intended that once the school for girls had been built, that the normal east west axis of the church would be assumed, ie the floor removed and the altar placed at the Washington Street end. When the parish was consulted, they preferred the present simple lines and so the liturgical south aisle and Holy Name Chapel were added in 1881 by way of enlargement, retaining the previous axis. The Annunciation window above the high altar was given in memory of Elizabeth Austin Attree, the first parishioner of the new church, wife of George Attree, who died in 1865, and whose family owned much of the land in the area. The window was designed by Edward Burne-Jones and executed by William Morris.

The first priests were the Reverend Charles Anderson, the Reverend Christopher Tompson - who stayed until 1875 and began the Sunday school, choir and the use of vestments - and Father George Chapman. Chapman was born in Liverpool in 1864 and arrived in Brighton to take up the post as priest at the Church of Annunciation in 1877, living at 85 Coleman Street. It must have been a very different living from that of his last parish of St James-the-Less in Liverpool, with about 10,000 parishioners of every European nationality, and well-nigh every religious denomination. Chapman was well thought of in the parish of Hanover, and highly respected by other clergy of the town because of his abilities as an evangelist, but he provoked antagonism among the town's low church faction by his extreme ritualism and love of Romish detail. His style of preaching was different from other Anglo-Catholic churches in Brighton and he actively discouraged middle class 'carriage folk' from visiting his church. Protestant protesters kept away from this very deprived area of town not wishing to tangle with the rough element of the area.

The dissenting minister, who had a chapel on the hill, said that the parish had a totally different appearance after Father Chapman had been there some time and showed his reverence by bringing a wreath of flowers to the church on the day of his funeral. Father Chapman was suceeded by the Reverend Reginald Fison, who carried on the good work of his predecessor, dying of typhoid in 1895 aged 42.

An observer at the time recalls "Within half an hour's walk of the fashionable parts of Brighton, halfway up a steep hill from the Lewes road, stands the Church of the Annunciation. The parish is compact, no house within it being more than five minutes walk from the church. Fifty years ago there were only a few houses scattered here and there among market gardens, made on the side of what once formed part of the Brighton Downs. Now there are 16 streets of small, modern houses for artisans; eight streets lie in parallel lines, intersected by the upward road. Many of the houses contain two or more families, while more than one of them are occupied by ladies who devote themselves to work amongst the poorer brothers and sisters."

There was one occasion, however, when some local people resorted to violence. The clergy and choir attempting to walk in procession through the parish were mobbed and an attempt was made to burn them by setting their surplices on fire.

Father Chapman died in 1891 of tuburculosis, aged only 44. It was difficult for anyone who was present at his funeral, and who witnessed the reverend order of the the dense crowd collected on that day, to believe the violence that had occurred on that eventful day some fourteen years previously.

Aubrey Beardsley

Aubrey Beardsley the artist, and his sister Mabel, chose to worship at the Church of the Annunciation, whilst living in Lower Rock Gardens. Beardsley forged a close bond with Father Chapman who became a father figure to him in the absence of his own. The Anglo-Catholic ritualistic ceremonies were to have a profound affect on Beardsley, who later became a Roman Catholic.

In 1898 The Archbishop of Canterbury declared the use of incense and portable lights within services to be illegal, and many clergy complied with this. The Annunciation was one of the few churches in Brighton where this prohibition was ignored.

Left: the Church of the Annunciation, built in 1864 and founded by the Reverend Arthur Douglas Wagner for the poor of Brighton. He was also the benefactor. In 1865 plans were lodged for the building of a Boys School in Southover Street, now the Community Centre

Below: interior of the Church of the Annunciation,

Belgrave Street Congregational Chapel c1910 on the corner of Belgrave Street and Southover Street. The Church of the Annunciation can be seen in the distance in Washington Street

Belgrave Street Congregational Chapel

Belgrave Street Congregational Chapel was erected by voluntary subscription. "a Place of Worship, part of which would be used as Day and Sunday School . . . Within a radius of about five hundred yards . . . were then residing more than two thousand families . . . nearly all of them being mechanics or day labourers. . . the building would principally be for the working classes. . . The population is still rapidly increasing." The infants school room was opened for public worship in 1859, the chapel and new school room were opened in 1863. "The chapel is divided from the school room by very large doors, removable at will, being on wheels - so as to throw all the building into one." In 1863 a class room and reading room - intended for the Brighton Working Men's Union - were added.

Recently the building had been used by the University of Brighton as a sculpture studio, but in 1999 permission was granted to convert it to housing. *Below: elevation facing Belgrave Street*

Bentham Road Mission

I come from a family of seven and attended the mission with my brothers and sisters between 1927 & 1935. You entered at the front of the building and to your right were stairs leading to a balcony. You walked through a doorway and you were in a large hall where all the services were held including the children's Sunday school. The boys and girls sat at opposite sides of the hall on oak forms arranged in a square, with a teacher for different age groups. When we gathered together for general assembly, the forms were arranged in rows across the hall. This was for the Sunday evening meetings for adults, harvest festivals, magic lantern shows and various other events.

There was an organ which one of the teachers played whilst working a pedal. Around the walls hung framed texts on a white background with blue lettering, and two marble plaques. Standing either side of the hall were two large round cast iron stoves, which in winter were very welcome.

Passing through the main hall there was a door which led to a smaller hall where the younger children were taught, also meetings of the Girls' Guildry, Girls' Life Brigade and Boys' Brigade. Adjacent to this hall was a passage way leading to a small flight of stairs leading to a small room which was used for a Bible class.

The mission is still standing. [It was opened as an infant school in 1896]. There were quite a few church halls and missions in the Hanover area run by kind people who fulfilled a need of the poor of that time, especially the children who were given prizes for good attendance. We had an annual Sunday school outing to Burgess Hill, the highlight of the year.

F E Smith and P Brooker nee Hedgecock

Ebenezer Baptist Chapel, Richmond Street, known as the Lemon Squeezer

Below: Ebenezer Baptist Chapel in 1960, demolished in 1965

I attended the Ebenezer Chapel Sunday School in Richmond Road and occasionally St Peter's Church. We were Church of England but the Ebenezer was nearer to our house. If you attended regularly you got points towards the summer outing which was usually to Victoria Gardens in Burgess Hill or to Hassocks. Pastor Kemp was in charge of us and Mr Spooner the caretaker also came. At Victoria Gardens there was a coconut shy and we would ask 'Daddy' Spooner as he was known, to take our turn because he was so good.

The people at the Ebenezer were very kind to the poor in the area, they would loan you a clean blanket for one shilling and you could keep it all winter; when you returned it you could get your shilling back and they would wash it ready for next year. My family didn't have to do that because we were fairly well off compared to many in the neighbourhood.

Mrs. Connie Dowds nee James

I attended the Ebenezer Chapel and if you read the lesson you got a Liquorice Allsort.

Pauline Hastings-Smith

Islingword Road Mission

The Trustees of the Primitive Methodist Church bought the plot of land in Islingword Road in 1881 and built an iron church. They sold it in 1892 and the Islingword Road Mission opened in 1893. Five years later the building was found to be dangerous and services were transferred to Finsbury Road school and the building rebuilt as it is today. The first service held in the new building was in 1899. In 1990 the name 'Mission' was felt to be old fashioned and it was called 'Islingword Road Evangelical Free Church'. The building celebrates its centenary in 1999.

I was taken to the Mission by my parents over eighty years ago when just a baby. No one who went to the Mission will ever forget the summer and winter treats. They were a triumph of organisation with Mr Groves at the helm. About seven hundred people, adults and children went for the day to Burgess Hill Pleasure Gardens by special train from Brighton station. The children marched in orderly fashion - banners and flags flying - down Islingword Road, along Lewes Road to Trafalgar Street. There was great excitement on the train journey and we couldn't wait to get into the Pleasure Gardens and book a boat on the lake. After a lovely tea Mr Groves would ring the hand bell around the grounds for everyone to make their way to the station and return.

The winter treat was held at the Mission and there was a prizegiving and a Magic Lantern show which consisted of animated animal pictures followed by slides of the summer treat.

Olive and Bernard Pelling

It was just fifty two years ago that I first entered the doors of Islingword Road Mission, a place that was to become my second home. The Sunday school was large with over two hundred pupils, ranging from under fives in the side room to two Bible classes, the girls upstairs and the boys downstairs. On one Sunday a month there was church parade when the uniformed organisations and the rest of the Sunday School marched around the streets with a band and a banner with 'Islingword Road Mission' on it. This was a witness and children would tag on from the streets.

Monday night was Girl Crusaders and we had a uniform of a white blouse with a green scarf, skirt and beret. I felt so proud wearing this as it made me equal with the other girls. Sometimes, during the winter evenings we met at 'Tindale' at 180 Freshfield Road, the home of Mr and Mrs Waldron, where we did handicrafts, such as painting glasses for presents. It was lovely there with a nice coal fire and so homely. In the summer we sometimes went to the Racehill for stoolball or rounders. Every year we gave a display of marching, dumbells, skipping and physical activities for parents and friends. I can also remember going with Miss Waite on a Saturday afternoon to entertain the old people in Brighton General Hospital.

Those early days were during wartime, when we experienced a lot of poverty; the Church supplied our physical as well as our spiritual needs.

Betty Gillett

St Joseph's church and school rooms in Milton Road, at the junction with Elm Grove in 1973. It was erected in 1869 for the Irish soldiers stationed in Brighton, but after the opening of the permanent church in Elm Grove this building continued to be used as a school and a church hall. It has since been extended and reconstructed.

Phoenix Brewery

The Phoenix Brewery

Richard Tamplin, a mercer born in Dane Hill, moved to Brighton in 1811, and by 1820 he was trading as the Sussex County Bank of Castle Square with Creasy, Gregory and Company. In the same year he purchased a small brewery in Southwick from Nathaniel Hall, which was destroyed by fire shortly afterwards. In spite of suffering an uninsured loss of over £10,000 Tamplin appears to have taken temporary premises in Worthing before beginning to build a new brewery in Brighton. The plans were drawn up the following year by the architect Henry Wilds, and the foundation stone was laid by Henry Pagden Tamplin, the brewer's eldest son.

It was this building, rising from the ashes, albeit on a different site, that became the 'Phoenix', soon to be the largest brewery in the county. By 1902 Tamplin's had occupied an area of 100,000 square feet bounded by Albion Street, Albion Hill, Newhaven and Southover Streets, employing 150 men. The Tamplins lived in a spacious house, at 1-3 Lennox Terrace, later Richmond Terrace, which became the company's offices. The counting house was a smaller red brick building at the entrance to the yard.

Richard Tamplin was partnered by his son Henry Pagden Tamplin, who after learning the trade, inherited the business on his father's death in 1849. Henry in turn was partnered by his eldest son William Cloves Tamplin, who inherited the business in 1867. So as to provide for his family of ten children, William transferred the business, valued at over £300,000 into a limited company in 1889, appointing himself as chairman. William commanded the First Volunteer Battalion of the Royal Sussex Regiment and his colonel built a drill hall in Church Street Brighton at his own expense, which, with its fine doorway, is still there today. William died in 1893 leaving an estate worth over £200,000 and absolute control of the brewery passed out of the family.

The business expanded with the acquisition of the licensed houses of several smaller concerns. In 1892 the nearby Albion Brewery in Albion Street was purchased and the premises were retained as a wine, spirit and bottled beer store. In 1899 the number of outlets was increased with the acquisition of the licensed houses of the Catt family.

The next year saw the purchase of the twelve houses of the Brighton Brewery Company from R C Weeks, a brewery in Osborne Street, Hove. It was used as a store for a short time before being demolished. In the same year the business of the South Malling Brewery at Lewes was purchased from Bishop & Son. Eventually Tamplins owned 200, over two thirds, of the licensed premises in the Brighton area, with a further 400 elsewhere.

Tamplins were taken over by the Watneys in 1953 although the business continued unchanged for a while. The last brew was in 1973, and the brewery was demolished in 1980, although much of the bottling and storage building remained until recently, while the site was retained as a depot before operations were transferred to Lewes.

The last of the brewing buildings have now gone and the site is used for housing, although the red brick office and houses in Richmond Terrace, including numbers 1-3, have been retained. The name 'Phoenix' was revived recently on many of the public house signs, replacing the earlier 'Red Barrel', although there are still many old premises that state 'Tamplin's Entire' on the walls.

I attended St Luke's school until I was fourteen and then went to work for Tamplin's Brewery. I worked from 5.30 am until 5.30 pm Monday to Friday and 5.30 am until 12 noon on Saturdays. I started each day by lighting the eight fires in the offices on the corner of Phoenix Place. The chemists who tested the beer worked there and I had to clean the grates and relay all the fires so that it was warm for them when they started work. At 8 am I had half an hour break in the back room to eat my sandwich. My main job then started in the tun room, where the bog vats were. The vats were green after the beer had been emptied from them and had to be cleaned. I had to get into the tuns and clean them with bundles of steel wool and pumice powder. After two weeks my hands were like raw meat but they gradually got used to it, and for this I received 10 shillings a week.

They kept three pairs of horses and wagons at the back which were used to deliver the barrels to the pubs.

Gordon Harwood.

When I left school at fourteen I went to work for Tamplin's Brewery. I worked in the tun room and wore an apron and wellington boots. I had to climb into the big tuns and with a wire brush and a hose pipe. I had to scrub all the pipes until they came up like brass. During the war we were bombed and we all dived underneath the barrels for protection. There was quite a lot of damage. I had to change to do war work when I was old enough and left Tamplin's to work for Allen West, the engineering firm in Lewes Road.

Mrs Vera Saunders

I came to Tamplin's in 1962 from the parent company Watney Mann. Tamplin's was still trading under its own name, and continued to do so until the end of the sixties. Tamplin's had a bottling store at Cannon Place and Russell Street until the land was purchased for Churchill Square. In 1964 a new bottling store was built on the Phoenix Brewery site and operated until its closure in the early seventies. The end of 1973 was a sad time for Tamplin's for it saw the end of brewing. The Phoenix Brewery became a distribution depot with all products being brought in by trucker lorries mainly from Brick Lane, Isleworth, and Mortlake Breweries. The company name changed again, this time to Watney's Southern Ltd and the early eighties saw what was to become the final change, the Phoenix Brewery Company.

From 1962 to 1975 I worked as assistant transport manager. In the first two years I would start work at 7 am and during the summer period it was not unusual to work until 8.30 pm. The drayman (lorry drivers and their mates) were on overtime payment, and a common practice then was for pub landlords to give the drayman a full lunch and the crews worked their rounds so they could arrive at the pub where they knew they could get the best food.

There were approximately fifty delivery vehicles then employing around 110 men as some vehicles had three men to handle deep and difficult pub cellars. Those were the years of hard physical work, but years with good camaraderie and a happy working atmosphere. Then came a period of change, from 1965 a new system of payment was introduced for the draymen. This provided the delivery men with the opportunity to go home as soon as their day's work was completed; not surprisingly the late summer working hours ceased.

The work of the draymen was then heavy, physical and thirst making, quenched in most cases with beer. It was not unusual for a drayman to consume up to fourteen pints during the course of his work on a hot summer's day. They were also entitled to a two pint beer allowance each day in the brewery mess room. This ceased with the introduction of the breathalyser, improved mechanical handling and smaller containers. The days of hogsheads (54 gallon vessels) and barrels (36 gallons) had gone forever, to be replaced with metal containers of 22 and 11 gallons. I was offered redundancy and was pleased to accept it.

Michael Evans

I came to the Phoenix Brewery in 1952 as a professional brewer, becoming second brewer and eventually chief brewer. Each beer had its own recipe, and it was my responsibility to see that the ingredients were to hand and fed into the process at the right time. We used local barley from Lewes and hops from Kent, delivered to the brewery by road in hop pockets (sacks). We had about fifty men on the production side and had enormous tuns, large wooden copper lined vessels which could make between nineteen and 150 barrels of beer at a time. These had to be cleaned out with pumice stone after every process, which was very hard work. The brewery was closed in 1974, when it became a depot and I became depot manager. I retired in 1982. I look back at my time at the Phoenix with fond memories.

Derek Nelmes

Below: Phoenix Street. The Free Butt Inn is still a public house. The Brewery office is now listed, and is being converted into a community centre. All the houses on the site have been demolished except Phoenix Place.

Public Houses

Public houses in the Hanover area are as popular today as they were in the past. There was a beer house or inn on nearly every street corner. In 1867 there were five public houses in Southover Street, as there are today. In 1872 there were: five inns and three beer retailers and by 1879 there were eight inns - the Greyhound, and the Bricklayers Arms being next door to one another.

The public house at the top of Southover Street has recently lost its name, 'The Royal Exchange' and is now known locally as 'the pub with no name'. In the 1870s it was an inn, where travellers could stay.

The Sir Charles Napier public house has many framed memorabilia collected by the publican, Barry Hewland, on the walls.

Below: the Flowing Stream Public House 22/23 Newhaven Street closed in 1953.

The Fox Inn (see back cover)

The Fox Inn was the first public house to be opened in Southover Street in c1845, with Peter Phillips as the landlord. The rest of Southover Street was not developed until the 1850s and 60s. The Fox continued to be a public house until the 1920s when it was converted to houses.

My great grandmother Mary was in service in a grand house just outside Brighton. She became pregnant by her employer or his son, and a daughter Frances was born in 1850. Mary returned to Brighton and married John Page. The father of her daughter Frances, who had kept in contact with her, settled money on her and they bought the Fox Inn in Southover Street. Her daughter Frances, my grandmother, was brought up in The Fox, as well as in various cookshops and eating houses in the area. The original clock from The Fox Inn is still in the family.

Mrs. Sonia Waterton nee Sully

I was the landlord of the Albion Pub from 1966-1992. The area was being redeveloped when I took over. Richmond Heights was built by in '66 and Dinapore House was very run down. Chates Farm was allotments and workshops, but by 1981 the Chates Farm flats were there. The area has changed, houses have been converted into flats and there are now more owner-occupiers and students. We tried to be a family pub when there were families in the small houses and it was very friendly, but that generation has gone and the new occupants have got their own way of life.

Dennis Alderson

Group outing of the Obed Arms in 1934, on the corner of Dinapore Street and Albion Hill. Dinapore Street, named after a town in India involved in the Indian Mutiny of 1857, was built in c1860. Mrs Kate Parker nee Layshley stands on the left wearing a white hat and fur stole. Her parents Minnie and James Layshley, landlords, stand in the doorway holding their grandson Alan. Mrs Parker aged 90 still lives in Brighton and has happy memories of the Obed Arms. There was a small back room where darts and cribbage were played, and a front bar where men drank. All the beer came from the barrel.

The Live & Let Live public house on the corner of Dinapore Street and Richmond Street 1956. The barrier across Richmond Street, to stop runaway horses, had been there for many years,

Opposite: The Charles Napier, Southampton Street annual ladies outing 1929. Mrs 'Tottie' Edwards stands second from the right in the back row next to her friend Nancy Jones. In front of them is their friend Rene Spencer, all three lived in Southampton Street

Two World Wars

First World War

The First World War affected most people who lived in the close-knit community of Hanover. Father William Carey was the incumbent of the Church of the Annunciation during the years of the First World War and he kept up a correspondence with members of the congregation.

France 1915 : George Strong, 1st Sussex Battery

"How is everybody at the dear old Annunciation? I hope you get good congregations at Mass on Sundays, although I expect you get fewer men. We don't go to church now, as we are not allowed near the church; but we generally have a service in our canteen. Jack sent me the June Parish magazine. I hear all the club chaps have joind the Army, and I should think the dear old Annunciation has contributed to the Motherland . . . Have you a Roll of Honour? Let me know how many are on it . . . I always think of the little church on the hill, and shall be very glad when the war is over and I can get back to those I love and all my dear friends."

Sapper Reg Hilder - wrote from Eastbourne.

"Well, I started soldiering properly now. There's rifle drill, trench digging, route marching with full kit, field geometry, hurdle-making, etc. It's quite a puzzle trying to get your kit together. Glad to say my arm is better now after inoculation, but each day brings the second dose nearer. I've met T Pelling up here as well as one or two other Annunciationites. It makes me feel more at home when we are all together. Tomorrow we get church parade at 9 am; it's a fine sight to see all the fellows and the band marching along to the church. I might say that we've got plenty of aeroplanes over here and an airship; these are flying from any time after 6 am."

October 1915 Jack Strong RAF France

"Just a line to thank you for the crucifixes. I have given them both away, and the chaps who received them, wish to thank you . . . for them . . . could you send me a song book to help us keep merry? I have got a wooden crucifix which I found in a village destroyed by the Germans, which I will send home to you at the first opportunity."

1916 Jack Strong OHMS

"There were some of the Royal Sussex Regiment in the village and I ran across one of the old Annunciation boys . . . my old chum Percy Nicholls. He was billeted in a village . . . close to where I am lodging in a railway tunnel, which are are draughty places to live in. . I have been in France over a year and consider myself to be an old soldier. I hear brother Reggie has had a turn in the trenches . . . I am on duty 'till 5 am so I can write some letters. We have a little dog which we keep as a mascot and have some fine sport with him as he is a fine rat-catcher. I heard from George recently who hopes to complete his tour round the world soon! We have a stream which runs close by so we can have a bathe, a luxury for us."

Annunciation Sunday School Recruiting March 7 November 1915

We did not touch the borders of the Parish. Our route lay through Hanover Terrace along Howard Road to Elm Grove and back again via Hampden Road, Islingword, Ewart and Jackson Streets and so on into Church.

It was clear from the start that if we did nothing else we would rouse the Parish. Boys hovered like bees around the band. People stood and watched us in the street; while some followed. Doors and windows opened and men were roused from their Sunday siesta to see us go by. Women, children and babies in arms were among the spectators. At the corner of the 'Island' in Islingword Road we called a halt and after a recruiting speech and a hymn, we marched on again along Islingword Street. Back in church we had a short service and sifted out the recruits and took their names and addresses. There were fifty-two in all.

However, when Sunday came, not all our recruits arrived, others, not reckoned with, put in an appearance. We had at least forty children, which was not bad.

Reverend Basil Shelley, assistant priest.

Street party to celebrate the jubilee of George V in 1935, outside 31 Toronto Terrace.

Second World War

Tuesday September 24 1940

Albion Hill and its surrounding area was hit by two heavy calibre bombs. One landed at the junction of Albion Hill and Ashton Street, demolishing a butcher's shop and killing the owner William Chubb. Nellie Vincent of 13 Albion Hill, aged 57, was pulled from the wreckage alive but died from her wounds in hospital. Cambridge and Ashton Streets were badly hit by bombs. Nearly thirty houses were so badly damaged that thay had to be demolished. The bombs caused minor damage to houses in a quarter of a mile radius and the streets were littered with glass.

The raid started just after 3.30 pm without warning, lthough the bomber had been seen for several minutes and was easily distinguishable as a German raider. The second bomb landed in a garden which wrecked houses in Cambridge Street and Dinapore Street. An oil bomb fell close by and exploded, wrecking a house at the junction of Cambridge Street and Albion Hill; the houses on the opposite side of the road were covered in crude oil. Several streets had to be evacuated including the Phoenix Brewery, for which it is thought, the bombs were meant. Most of the injured were children who had not long been out of school and were playing in the streets.

In all thirty three houses were demolished as well as the Sir John Falstaff pub at 137 Albion Hill. Many families were sheltered at Congress Hall overnight, and they returned to salvage what belongings they could from the wreckage the following day, German fighters appeared overhead and machine gunned them. Terrified, they lay in the gutter and covered their heads with their hands.

During the war years, what is now the now Community Centre was taken over by the REME. I was engaged to a soldier training there. Enemy air raiders tried many times to set light to Tamplin's Brewery. Bombs hit the end of Lewes Street demolishing a paper shop and a huge piece of masonry crashed through our shop window. Luckily no one in our shop was hurt.

Eve King

Albion Hill bombed.

On the day in 1940 the bomb hit my aunt's shop. I was the only girl working at Blecos in St Martin's Place, making small parts for bombs. I had been there about three months and we were on the roof eating our sandwiches when we heard a plane overhead making a funny noise. We looked up in bright sunlight and Len Anscombe said "It's all right it's one of ours", and we could see the red, white and blue under the wings. It was flying north along Lewes Road, then it suddenly returned and we saw the swastikas on the wings, heard a terrible bang and saw clouds of smoke. A bomb had hit the Lewes Road Inn at the bottom of Franklin Road and Peter Williams the manager was killed. We went back into work and I was called to see the boss and given sweet tea. I was worried because I thought I'd done something wrong but they told me that my aunt's shop had received a direct hit. They sent me home in the firm's lorry.

We managed to get round by Phoenix Place, but when we got to the bottom of the hill it was devastated. I remember going up to the shop and I started screaming because I knew our house was next door. A Salvation Army lass came over and gave me some tea in a jam jar and they told me that my mother, sister, aunt and cousin had been taken to hospital. My father arrived, having seen the smoke of the bomb from the wall at Brighton station and thought it seemed near our home, which was badly damaged. Johnny Knight lived next door and I could hear a boy crying in the rubble. The men said they'd looked there but I said that I recognised his voice as he was Scottish. They started digging and I spotted his hand. They got him out but his legs were badly smashed. If I see him he always says "You saved my life". We were all taken to the Citadel by The Level where we were given blankets and hot cocoa and thick bread from Hobden's, the baker in London Road.

Seven members of my family were in Bristol ward at the Sussex County hospital. While they were there I went out dancing at Sherry's with a friend called Ruby Grinyer and on the way home there was an air raid. We rushed into what we thought was an empty house, but beyond the front door was a drop and I fell and injured my leg. I ended up in a camp bed on Bristol ward between my mother and grandmother.

The Ebenezer Chapel in Richmond Street (photograph on page 27), the Duke of Cambridge and the Lennox Arms pubs were bombed. I was asked to be an Air Raid Warden but I'd only been training for four weeks when we had a scare and had to go to the shelter between Albion Hill and Southover Street. The cement was still wet when we reached it but they had a 'phone and tea and a bucket behind the door in case we needed it. Albion Street was bombed in the war and all the little cobbled cottages went and they rebuilt the area with houses and flats.

Jackie Griffiths

The Newhaven Street area was bombed on my son Brian's seventh birthday. I was lying on my bed when my husband came in and said that Lewes Street and Dinapore Street had been bombed. Brian was at Richmond Street School and I ran over to my friend Win's house and shouted, "There's a bomb down the bottom of our street and the kids are in school". I only had slippers on but I ran all the way down the street to the school and saw a little girl lying on the step outside the Falstaff Pub in Albion Hill. Miss Coombs the headmistress met us and said, "The children are alright." So I went home and thought I'd better get my Brian's party ready.

Mrs Twell from Dinapore Street, who had six children, was blinded, and Mr Flood the butcher was killed. Then they came round and said we'd have to get out of our houses because a time bomb had been dropped on the brewery. I said "No, I'm not going, if it goes up I'll go with it". The next day my husband went for a drink and he rushed back and said "Get down here quick, they're just about to let the time bomb off". I jumped down the stairs from top to bottom.

Kathleen Lilley

Prefabricated houses on a bombed site

Above: victory celebration street party in Cambridge Street

Bombs affected the Chates Farm area badly. There was a butcher's shop that was absolutely flattened. My Uncle Bill worked at the shop but he was on an errand when the bomb dropped. Uncle Bill lived in Lewes Street and when he returned home he found his own house was blown to pieces and his daughter had been blown across the room out of her chair, but she survived. His family moved in with my grandparents in Grove Street and they were rehoused in Lincoln Street.

Roy Wilkinson

My dad was Chief Air Raid Warden for the Hanover Area. and used to run a club for the children of Hanover Ward. Parents paid a penny a week for each child and they had two really good parties a year, held in the Church of the Annunciation's halls. Everyone enjoyed themselves.

Mrs. J. Fennell

My stepfather ran a grocery shop at 32 Richmond Buildings. It was my job to cut out all the coupons, count them and send them to the Ministry of Food. I put my age up by a year so that I could join the Home Guard and I fire watched at the Royal Alexandra Hospital.

John Rackham

We lived at 58 Southampton Street, there were seven boys and four girls in the family. When the Second World War broke out all the boys enlisted, one into the Air Force and six into the Army. The Herald took our picture in the back yard, also of the Perin family opposite who had eight sons who enlisted. We were lucky, all seven of us returned from the war unhurt.

Frank Edwards

Schools

Education during the nineteenth century was mainly confined to the children of the wealthy, with working class children relying on a haphazard arrangement of Dame Schools, Sunday Schools and eventually Church Schools for their education.

As the population from Carlton Hill spilled into Hanover the demand for school places increased, the churches were quick to respond. The Belgrave Street Chapel School opened in 1863, swiftly followed by St. Mary's Boys School at the Church of the Annunciation in 1864. St. Joseph's School in Milton Road opened in 1874 to cater for the increase in Catholic families in the town.

The Education Act of 1870 enabled School Boards to be set up in districts where there were insufficient schools to cater for the number of children. During the next thirty years Thomas Simpson designed many of the Board Schools which still remain in use in Brighton today and make such notable punctuation marks in the townscape of Brighton.

Belgrave Street School (photograph and elevation page 26)

Belgrave Street School opened in 1859 with a school room, used as an Infants school and opened for public worship in the same year. The Congregational Church was active in poorer areas of the town and identified a need for a school in Hanover. Brighton School Board took control as soon as it was founded, and rooms at the Belgrave Street Chapel continued to be used as a small school until 1942, when it was closed and the children dispersed amongst other schools. The building later became an annexe to the University of Brighton, and is now being converted to housing.

St. Mary's Boys School, late School of the Annunciation (photograph page 25)

St. Mary's Boys school was opened in 1865 by the Reverend A D Wagner with twenty one boys, and it moved to Southover Street in 1872. The letters 'SM' can still be seen carved over the front entrance. It was known as St Paul's school when the Annunciation was served by curates from St Paul's church, it became the Annunciation School in about 1900, the Corporation's Handicraft school in 1924, the Southover Street Canteen - or soup kitchen as it was known in the 1930s, an education supply store after the war and is now the Hanover Community Centre.

During the 1870s the head was Cornelius Down who kept a log book of the school:

1871: a new window was being fitted into the school room causing disruption to school work:

4 August: assembled the school in classroom where we conducted the work as far as possible, on account of the noise. Attendance very good.

14 August: admitted two boys, found heat and dust from the road through open window very inconvenient for working satisfactorily.

25 August: Gave the first 3 Standard an examination in the 3 R's and found a few dull boys backward in arithmetic especially F Kent in 3rd Standard who appears to have no idea of figures.

1 September: Several boys absent this week through illness (diarrhoea)

11 September: Admitted four new boys, all very backward in their work.

4 October: School examined by HM Inspector's assistant. Presented nine boys.

St. Joseph's Roman Catholic School (photograph on page 29)

St. Joseph's Roman Catholic School, a small church school was opened in Milton Road in 1879 in premises built as a Church to cater for the Irish Catholic soldiers who were stationed in Brighton.

A band playing at St Joseph's School in Milton Road the1930s

The premises were small and the largest room was divided into four classrooms. As early as 1908 the Inspector was condemning the premises as being inadequate for the teaching of children, but Brighton Council was not prepared to pay for a new building. The school catered for children aged 5-14 but if the boys passed the scholarship examination at 11, they could go to Xaverian College in Queen's Park instead of Varndean Grammar School

The head of St Joseph's was a Miss Mattimore and her sister was the senior teacher; Miss Chapel ran the infants department in a classroom on its own. Other classes were taught together, with two rows of desks for one class and two for the other, with one teacher for both. One group would be taught whilst the other group got on with work and then the arrangement was reversed for the next lesson. The boys had to walk to Belgrave Street school to do carpentry, the girls walked to Montpelier Road for cookery classes, and both groups had to walk to and from the Wild Park for their physical education lessons.

The hours were 9 am-12 noon and 2-4 pm with a two hour break for lunch. There were no school meals so we all had to go home. The bell was rung to let us know when school was starting and ending. We had a small bottle of milk every day and when it was cold in the winter, a monitor would bring it in and put the crate near the fire to warm it up. Nurses, who we called 'Nitty Nora', came to inspect our hair and if you were found to have nits you had to stand in the playground until your mother came to collect you. Once a year a doctor came to measure and weigh you.

There wasn't very much space for the children at play time and the girls went into the small back garden whilst the boys played in Milton Road (not much traffic in the 1930s). There was a pub called the Elm Grove Tavern on the other corner of Milton Road and Elm Grove and the publican didn't like the boys playing in the road as he feared his windows would get broken. Eventually the school bought the house next door and we were able to use that garden as well.

Patrick Cheeseman & Margaret Miller

It was not until 1956 that the Church was able to fund a new school in Hollingdean, where St. Joseph's remains to this day.

Hanover Board School, Hanover Terrace

The Brighton & Preston Board School purchased land in Coleman Street and Hanover Terrace between 1872 and 1901 to build Hanover Terrace Board School. This area was described as lying in Islingword Furlong in Hilly Laine.

The school was opened in 1873. When the schools were reorganised in 1928, Hanover Terrace school became a Junior Mixed and Senior Boys' school only, while the Senior Girls and later the infants department, which closed in 1932, moving to other local schools.

During the Second World War numbers dropped dramatically and the the school was threatened with closure. It closed after the war and was used by the Secondary Technical school. Planning permission was granted in 1999 to replace the building with houses.

Above: sampler made by Emily Sims, born in 1867 in Boston Street, Brighton

I started at Hanover Terrace school when I was five. We didn't have bottles of milk or school dinners so we went home for dinner. The girl next to me was quite well off as she always had fruit to eat. The only time we had apples was when we went scrumping along the lane at the bottom of Southover Street where the tree hung over the wall.

I spent very little time in school as my mother was always ill and confined to bed so my father would say "You can't go to school today", because there was always a baby in the house and the boys didn't have to look after babies. I don't think I ever did a full week at school and I grew to loathe it because I was away so much I couldn't catch up. I used to think "Why should I learn about history when there are children to look after". I can remember coming out of my house in Hanover Terrace and bending low in front of our little wall, and looking up and down the street before I came out to see if the School Board Man was about. I dodged him most of the time but he caught me once. If my father had written a note it would have been alright. I used to get my knuckles rapped with a ruler because I was away so much, so I resented the school and authority.

Before I went to school I used to go to a fruiterer, Measors, at 114 Islingword Road, but they also sold coal. I used to get 28lb bag of coal on a trolley and wheel it down Southover Street so that we'd have coal for the day. I then lugged this coal sack into the house and put it into the cupboard in the passage and took the trolley back. This particular day I arrived at school with filthy hands and I was sitting in the front of the class when the headmistress came in. She said "How dare you come to school with such filthy hands, go and wash them immediately." All the children giggled when I returned to the class. Miss Long, who was teaching us that day, said "How many of you children helped your mothers this morning? You all laughed at Dorothy Page, but she gets up early and fetches coal for her mother."

We had to have plimsoles for sport as we normally wore heavy boots, but I hadn't any plimsoles. We all said we forgotten them and for that we would get a whack across the hand.

Dorothy Farrell nee Page, deceased

I passed the scholarship for Varndean but my parents couldn't afford to send me, as we had to pay for our own paper, pencils, and uniform and my father had retired from his railway job.

Jackie Griffiths nee George

Richmond Street Board School

Richmond Street Board School was opened in 1873 and with Hanover Terrace school served a large, mainly poor catchment area. The school ran from Richmond Street to Sussex Street fronting Claremont Row. It was an imposing building which stretched along the whole of the street with the Girls School at the Richmond Street end and the Boys School at the Sussex Street end. The playgrounds separated the two schools which overlooked the houses in Ivory Place.

The school was amalgamated with Circus Street school in 1927 and they were known as the Sussex Street schools. In 1959 the area came under a Compulsory Purchase Order, Richmond Street was demolished although the Circus Street school building is still used by the University of Brighton.

Brighton Education Committee School Building Annual report 31.3.1911: Arrangements are to be made for the feeding of necessitous school children at Richmond Street, Park Street and Elm Grove in the winter and at Richmond Street in the summer.

1912: Breakfast is to be provided for poor children during the Christmas and Easter holidays which will consist of hot milk and buns.

H M I Report Sussex Street Schools January 1925: The social conditions of the neighbourhood greatly influence the curriculum and aims of teaching in this school. A large share of the teachers' efforts must necessarily be given to the general training of the girls, arousing healthy ambitions, directing effort and developing self control, while all suffer from restricted opportunity and outlook. Much has been done to secure cleanliness and to encourage self-respect. The retarded need more specialised treatment than can be given in an ordinary elementary school.

H M I Report Sussex Street Schools 1927: Boys generally behave well and showed willingness during the inspection. Standard 10 however too readily became playful.

H M I Report Sussex Street School Junior Mixed 1930: Two classes have over 50 pupils. Training in good social habits.

H M I Report Sussex Street Schools Infants 1934: Since this school is situated in a district where the mothers need all the help that can be given them, a Nursery class was formed in October 1930 with 17 children aged 3 years which has now increased to 37 children. There is also a transition class of 40 four year olds. They enjoy free activity and sleep and are taught good habits, cleanliness, self help, obedience and good temper in play.

I went to Richmond Street Infants school which was just opposite our shop so I didn't have to go far. Every afternoon we would be put on our little beds for a sleep. There was an old sink with goldfish in it which I enjoyed looking at. Of course the toilets were outside. Later I transferred to Circus Street school but had to be transferred to St John's when it closed down.

Mrs. Connie Dowds nee James

We would come down Richmond Street and climb over the wall of the Girls School to take a short cut through their playground to the Boys School. As Richmond Street was a steep hill you could look through the railings into the bedrooms of a row of cottages in Ivory Place below. Mothers could pass food through the railings to their children in the playground.

Charles (Jim) Moore.

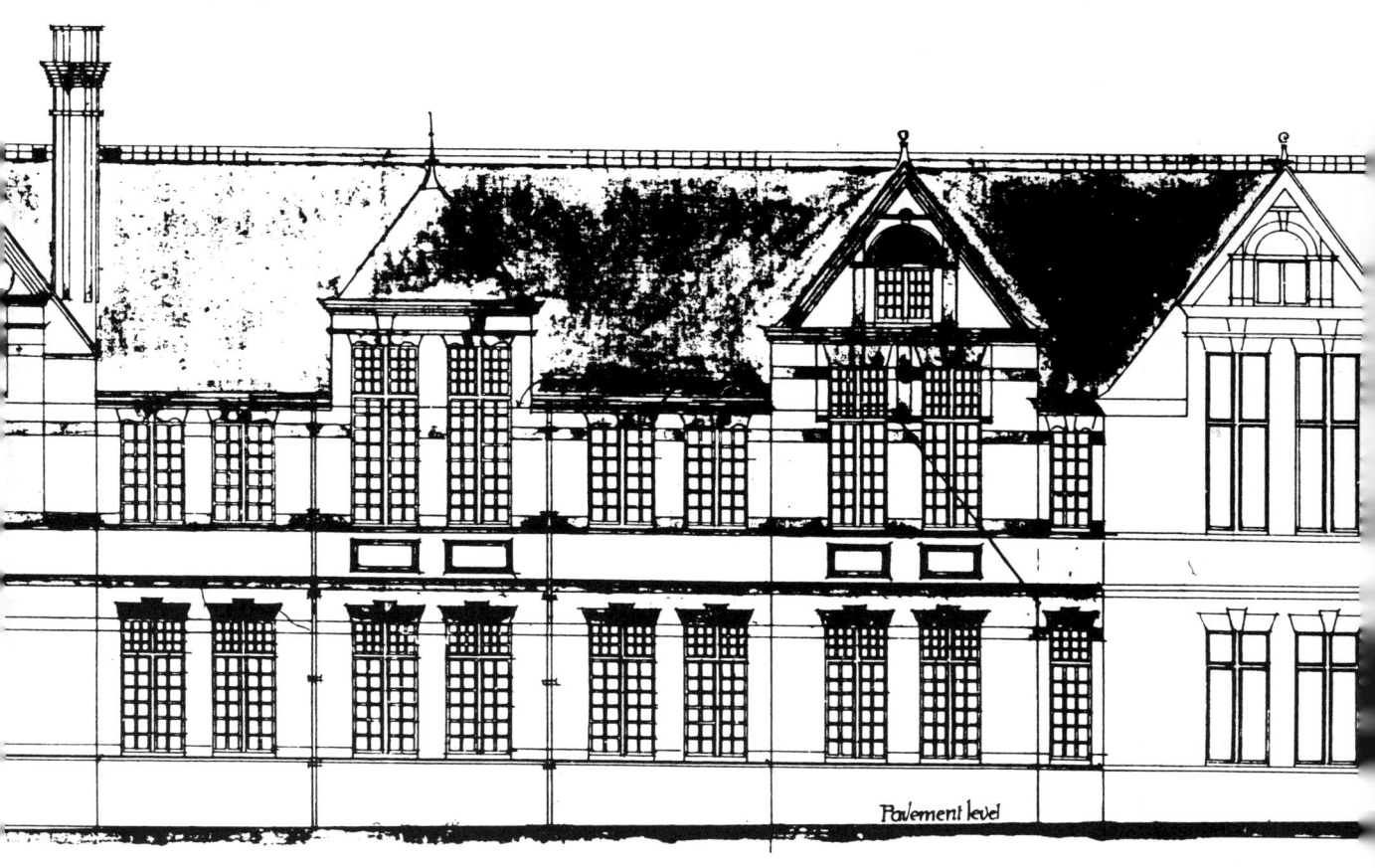

Finsbury Road Board School. *Above: proposed alterations to the original building 1903*

Finsbury Road Board School was opened in 1881 and in 1903 the pupils were transferred to the new St Luke's school whilst alterations were made. The school reopened in 1904 and as Bentham Road Infants school had closed, these children were transferred to Finsbury Road school. It became an Infants and Junior Mixed school from 1928, the senior pupils being transferred to other schools. The Infants school closed in 1955 and the Junior Mixed school closed in 1956. The premises were used by St Luke's school and then became a Brighton Polytechnic Annexe, later an annexe of the University of Brighton. In 1999 the University applied for planning permission to demolish the school and replace it with housing. The building was subsequently listed as of architectural and historical interest and the University then applied for permission to convert it to flats.

H M I Report February 1908: The influence of the school is a healthy one and the girls are carefully trained in the right habits, but in some classes might be rather more alert and ready in response. The curriculum includes reading, recitation, composition, arithmetic, history and geography. The Infants are carefully trained in habits of neatness and of cheerful obedience. This was practically a new school three years ago and was not very fortunate in the boys who were drafted into it on its reopening.

H M I report Junior Mixed 1930: The largest class was fifty nine pupils as there was a bulge of ten year olds. Too much needlework is attempted in the top classes.

I went to Finsbury Road, but had cooking lessons at Elm Grove school. My father was sometimes out of work and I would receive tickets for food and have free school meals at Elm Grove.

Mrs. Harriett Waldron

My grandfather Monk used to work for Carter Patterson Carriers delivering wines, spirits, gas and paraffin stoves from the station. He had a horse drawn cart with a 'dickie seat'. The horse was stabled in the station yard and if he had deliveries in the Finsbury Road area at 4.30 pm he would reach across with his whip to tap at the classroom window and take out his watch to show the teacher the time. Miss Hills, the teacher, used to say "Your grand-daughter has two minutes to go" and he would say "Right I'll come and fetch her then" at which point I would be allowed to leave. I would sit on the back of the cart with my legs dangling and get a lift home.

Jackie Griffiths nee George.

I was born in Montreal Road in 1926 and lived there until 1948. I attended Finsbury Road school from the age of four. The school was divided into Infants, Junior Mixed and Senior Girls. Mr Tierney, the caretaker, lived in a house next to the boys' entrance at 59 Southampton Street which had a door from his garden leading to the playground. Needless to say we had outside toilets.

There were quite a lot of poor children from large families, especially in Southampton Street, and sometimes they had very little in the way of clothes and shoes.

Scholarship examinations were taken at aged 10 or 11 over two days at Park Street school. We were given a pen and ruler to take with us and told if we lost them we would have to pay for them. If you passed the examination you could go to the Intermediate school in York Place and if you passed with exceptionally high marks you took another examination to go to Varndean school.

Cookery classes were held at Sussex Street school and later at Pelham Street school. Netball, hockey etc. were played at Moulsecoomb playing fields just past the barracks. We walked there in crocodile and those lucky enough to have a penny could catch the tram home.

In 1939 there were only 100 girls in the school and it was decided to close it and I finished my last three terms at Elm Grove, some of it part time, as by now the evacuees were arriving from London and the school was shared.

Mrs. E. Campbell nee Boyett.

I attended Finsbury Road school until I was fourteen. The school bell rang when school was about to start but on the way there I would be sent to a shop in Islingword Road, now a Post Office, where they would accept bets, illegal then. My dad would write down a bet and say "As you run round the corner just call in with this." I didn't like doing this and would insist that it would make me late for school but he would say "No you won't, just run." I'd put my head round the door and say "Dad said ...", leave the bet and run off to school as the bell was ringing.

Mrs. Vera Saunders

Elm Grove Board School *Photograph taken in 1905*

Elm Grove Board School opened in 1893 when over 300 children from Bentham Road Infants school were transferred, but by the end of the summer term the school role had risen to 800, including 438 infants. From 1928 the site was occupied by Senior Girls, Junior Mixed and Infants; the Senior Boys being dispersed to other schools. In spite of a fear that the school might be closed in the 1980s when the numbers attending fell, Elm Grove still remains as a primary school and is the only original Board School to remain in use in the area.

H M I Report 1904: Boys are carefully taught, discipline excellent, singing extremely well taught, drawing good. Girls - good methods are adopted in instruction and thoroughly satisfactory results are consequently obtained. Jessie Bevis employed as a monitress in the Infant Department at two shillings a week.

H M I Report 1905: Girls - The school is overfull and there are not sufficient desks for all the children.

H M I Report 1913: Boys - The syllabus in history, geography & science is above the heads of the boys. The teachers have become lecturers, boys listeners. French has been withdrawn from the timetable and science much reduced.

Girls - High estimate on manners and behaviour but considerable weakness on the intellectual side. Attainments of the girls are far too much on the surface and rest upon no solid foundation.

H M I Report 1921: Boys - industrious and respond readily. Only twenty of the 186 eligible boys can at present attend the Handicraft Centre.

Girls - Pleasant and happy conditions but disappointed that none of the girls reached the Ex V11th Standard. English well done, arithmetic weaker.

Bentham Road School (plan on page 27)

Bentham Road School opened in 1896 in a church building which consisted of one large hall with three classrooms and the usual outbuildings. Twenty nine children were admitted during the first week ages between three and four years, none of whom knew the alphabet. On 19 June ten more children had been admitted but all were backward. The elder children were working with them to teach them the alphabet and short words.

In 1896 there were many cases of whooping cough and there was some absence when the weather was bad, but the class sizes had increased to seventy one. Some children were transferred to Elm Grove as the numbers grew but the Inspector's Report in 1898 stated that: "These are inconvenient premises and the Board will I trust erect suitable permanent buildings as speedily as are practicable. Discipline is excellent." In 1899 the Inspector was still pressing for new premises and the north end class room was now used for mothers' meetings during the week.

In 1901 there was a great deal of sickness amongst the children, with such large classes the infections spread quickly. When the school reopened after the summer holidays a notice was received from the Medical Officer of Health to exclude all children from Islingword and Southampton Streets because of an epidemic of diptheria.

In 1902 sixty children went from the school to have boots fitted, a present from the 'New Tears Dinner & Boot Fund' Committee. The Inspector still complained about the unsuitable premises but to no avail. In 1904 a strongly worded report was sent to the School Board: "It behoves the Education Authority of the Borough to remove young children speedily from unsuitable, unhygienic premises." Bentham Road School was finally closed in 1904 and the children transferred to Elm Grove and Finsbury Road schools.

In 1906 the Education (Provision of Meals) Act was brought in and the Education Committee provided meals in the areas where they felt it was necessary.

The state system of school medical inspections began as a result of the Education (Administrative Provision) Act 1907. This enabled medical inspections of children immediately before, or at the time, or as soon as possible after, admission to the school. Attendance on the days of the medical inspections was found to be very low.

Under the Employment of Children Act 1910, the Inspectors in Brighton found that 1683 boys and 265 girls were illegally employed out of school hours. The worst schools included: Richmond Street Girls 52, Finsbury Road Girls 44. Hanover Terrace Boys 108 and Girls 10. Jobs they were employed in included working in barber's shops and licensed houses. 71 boys and 8 girls worked on milk or paper rounds and 160 boys worked as errand boys. 20 boys and 1 girl were found to be employed after 9 pm and many girls under 10 found employment such as minding a baby or running errands, often unpaid.

Laundries

The area of Hanover, like many other working class areas, saw numerous hand laundries set up in small terraced houses to enable women to supplement the often meagre wages of the men. Many jobs, such as building, declined in winter and women often had to find ways to keep the family fed and clothed. Laundry work was dominated by married or widowed women, could be adapted to fit in with domestic responsibilities and was unusual in that it could be carried out over a lifetime. .

In the 1851 census Hanover Street had sixty eight households and twenty women, including nine widows, involved in laundry work. Hanover Terrace had fifty seven households, including forty two laundresses, four of whom are quoted employing other women, with five ironers. Contemporary maps show that there were laundry fields on the slope behind Hanover Street, and this facility combined with the opportunities for obtaining work from the middle class developments of Hanover and Park Crescents would have made the area attractive to women who needed to make a living.

Some of the hand laundries developed into larger concerns, like the Cobden Road Hand Laundry, which employed about six women from the area, and Gochers in Islingword Road which was mechanised and still remains in business today.

Cobden Road Hand Laundry. Granny Pelham is standing in the doorway while her husband rests in a chair

My great grandmother had a hand laundry at 25 Cobden Road. Granny Pelham was my father's side of the family so I do not know much about her, but I have a faded laundry list and a photo of her outside the house with the washing drying outside.

Mrs. Jean Edwards

Gocher's Laundry, Islingword Road, in the 1960s

My maternal grandmother, Ann Shepherd aged twelve, was sent to Brighton from Barcombe Mills to work at her aunt's laundry at 29 Henry Street. She married Arthur Berry in 1891 when she was twenty and he was twenty two. Arthur was a jolly man who liked a drink and the races and always dressed in a brown suit and bowler hat. He was a general labourer, but my grandmother, who was trained in laundry work, decided to run a laundry from her home to supplement their income. They moved to Sutherland Road in 1891, and later to 4 Toronto Terrace, where a laundry called the Imperial Laundry had already been established by a Mrs Scarterfield. My mother's brothers were all a dab hand at ironing and Arthur had a handcart with which he collected and delivered the laundry.

Unfortunately Arthur died in 1915 aged forty five, leaving my grandmother to bring up the family with the proceeds from the laundry. She employed several women and was very upset when the law changed and she had to pay women's insurance stamps. After the war she married the man next door who was a gardener. She sold the laundry in 1926/7 and moved to Hollingdean.

Mrs Jennifer Besbrode

There were times when my father was out of work and we relied on my mother's cleaning job at the hospital in Elm Grove and the nurses' washing she brought home. She would scrub all evening. There was a long stool in the scullery and in the corner a copper and two big wooden tubs. Dad made her a long ironing board and she put the big black iron on the grate to heat up.

Sometimes I would be sent to the to the jug and bottle department at the Sir Charles Napier pub in Southover Street to buy a drink for my grandmother. I could see women in the pub, who I thought looked rather rough, who wore caps and coarse aprons. I think they worked in the laundries in Finsbury Road opposite the 'bad girls home' [Church Army Home for Girls].

Mrs. Harriett Waldron nee Read

I was born at 13 Arnold Street and was the youngest of four girls. I attended Elm Grove School and left when I was 14. The school didn't help me get a job but it was important that we started work as soon as possible. My mother went to Mrs Eves who ran a small hand laundry at 2 Arnold Street and asked if she had any vacancies. I left school on the Friday and started at Mrs Eves on the Monday, ironing handkerchiefs all day with a big metal iron that you heated on a stove. I worked from 8 am - 6 pm for five shillings a week and stuck it for a year. One of my older sisters worked at a laundry, she put in a word or me and I started with her for 25 shillings a week.

Mrs Betty Ticehurst

COBDEN LAUNDRY,

44, COBDEN ROAD, ELM GROVE, BRIGHTON.

Entirely under New Management. For "PRIVATE FAMILIES ONLY."

No other class of Washing Undertaken.

MRS. M. BRISLAND, *Proprietress.*

I left St. John's school in Carlton Hill in the early 1930s aged fourteen and went to work in the Model Laundry in Brading Road, which was run by a Mr Farlington. I went to this laundry as women neighbours of ours in William Street worked there. I received 7/6d a week for working 8 am - 8pm Monday and Tuesday when all the laundry came in and needed sorting for washing, and 8 am - 6 pm for the three other days - sorting, marking, racking, pressing, folding and using the hydro - a drier that spun the washing. The blankets would be hung out or put in drying rooms. Quite a lot of people in the street worked at the laundry.

There were a lot of hand workers who starched collars and polished the machines. At Gochers laundry we had presses, we had one the shape of a man's leg that we pulled men's woollen socks over to keep their shape, and we sent some of the ironing out to women in their own homes. It was mostly girls who worked in the laundry, except for a couple of maintenance men who turned down the steam from the calender when it got too hot. We used the calender - like a mangle - for the big sheets. Two people stood in front feeding in the sheets and two stood behind to collect them. We wore white starched overalls and it was terribly hot when all the machines were working, although we always had the windows open and the fans going. On Thursdays everything would go to the packing room where it would be sorted into pigeon holes using the laundry mark, ticked off in the customers book and tied into a brown paper parcel for delivery by van. The staff rest room was underground and very dark and I didn't like to sit down there during my lunch hour. There was always a good atmosphere in the laundry with the other girls and we sometimes had a sing song. I belonged to the 'perm club' where we contributed 6d a week and every week we had a draw to see who would get the 8/6d for their perm.

Later I went to work at Cobden Road Hand Laundry. This wasn't as mechanised as Gochers but I really liked it and the owner was a lovely person. Miss Winder did the hand washing - the woollens, silks and delicates, and they were hung out to dry in the garden or, if the weather was bad, they would be put on lines around a coke boiler to dry. Each of us had two hand irons on the go at a time, one would be round the coal fire stove heating up while the other was in use. It wasn't until later that gas irons were used.

I left the hand laundry when I married and I think they were sorry to see me go.

Mrs Roseann West nee Green

When my husband was made redundant as a British Rail driver we had to find another way of bringing in an income. I heard from a school friend that her grandmother, Mrs Bellchamber, who had been at school with my grandfather, wanted to retire from the laundry in Cobden Road opposite the Cobden Arms, so we bought her business.

It wasn't a trade that you liked, but you had to make a living and we stayed there for twenty eight years. It was called the 'Cobden House Hand Laundry', but we dropped the 'Hand Laundry' when we had our first washing machine. There were other laundries in the street which looked like private houses, but there was a roller shuttered entrance at the side of ours which lead to a large piece of level land with apple and pear trees, which was used for drying blankets and other washing.

We had eight staff, four washers and four ironers. The ironers were on the ground floor with the washing area behind. The ironers worked from Tuesday to Friday from 8 am - 4.30 pm with an hour for lunch. The packers were on the first floor where they had racks where the clothes were sorted. On Friday morning the clothes would be collected from the rack, checked against the laundry books, and packed into a neat brown paper parcel for delivery on Saturday. We lived in the flat on the second floor. There was no machinery at first, but we gradually mechanised with roller machines and a 'hydro' for drying and electric irons. Originally we had a big iron stove with four tiers which would heat up 100 irons. We were governed by the 'Factory Act', so we had inspectors to look at our machines. We had ironing machines for handkerchiefs, pillow cases and towels and revolving lathes overhead for the washing machines. All the small laundries helped each other, if our driver was out another would help.

On Mondays my husband collected the dirty laundry with laundry marks in red cotton. We took whites, cottons, woollens and silks. The sheets, pillow cases and towels would all go into the washing machine. If we had too much to cope with we would ask another laundry to help, we never turned work away. The Tivoli laundry in Crescent Road would take up to 100 sheets and Gochers sometimes helped. Miss Tarner of Tarner Nursery fame was among our customers, as was Mrs Allen West [the wife of the director of the Allen West factory in Lewes Road] who lived at The Drive in Hove. We had four rounds in Brighton.

We had a loyal staff, mainly elderly local women, all except the driver who was always a man. It was hard work and there was a lot of steam especially when the copper was boiling and the ironers got steam from the wash room because it was at the same level.

By the 1950s everything changed with the introduction of washing machines.

Laundry owner

THE QUEEN'S PARK
LAUNDRY & CLEANING WORKS

(Established 28 Years),

31, TORONTO TERRACE, QUEEN'S PARK, BRIGHTON.

—:o:—

Proprietor—MR. HENRY CURCHOD.

Manageress Laundry Department—MRS. HENRY CURCHOD.

—:o:—

Street Life

Chate's Farm

Chate's Farm was built on Tarner's land and the farmers were all tenant farmers, as were the Chate family, who were dairy farmers who also sold eggs and rhubarb. Before the 1914-18 war George, the son, had a milk business in Hamilton Road. He had to get rid of it in the war as he was called up, but after the war he bought a shop in Windmill Terrace selling milk, eggs, butter and cheese. George sold his business when the Co-op came into the area to deliver milk.

Our parents became tenants of the Chates in the 1930s. When we moved into the farm house as children the farm buildings were being used as workshops and garages and were surrounded by the farm which backed onto Liverpool Street. Milk was still being sold, served from the 'Can House', reached by a little path along which people would come with their jugs. We now use this building for our washing.

Mr. Chate retired from work at the age of forty to look after his ill wife. He moved with his wife and daughter in to a bungalow which he built in the garden. It was bought by the council after their death. We would have liked to move in, but the council decided to put a family with many children in it. When they left it was so badly damaged it had to be demolished.

We could sit at the side of the house in the evenings and look across Brighton; it was a marvellous view. All that changed in the 1960s when they demolished much of the area and they built an enormous block of flats which blocked our view.

Below: Thornsdale flats being built in 1960, taken from Highleigh. Chate's Farm is on page 55

The Tarners sold their land bit by bit. A planning application was submitted to build a block of flats, now called 'Chate's Farm Court' where the old farm buildings were. We objected to the original plan because the spur of the flats would have been right in front of us. Fortunately they changed the plan so we still have some of our view left. When they came to build the flats the slight camber on the farm land made a big drop into Liverpool Street and to save putting a lift in the flats they built them on two levels with access from both sides.

Ralph and Daphne Howard

Chate's farm supplied most of the milk in the area. It arrived in churns and you could get a jug for one shilling and tuppence. During the war bombs affected the Chates Farm area badly.

Roy Wilkinson

I lived at 80a Richmond Street opposite Chate's Farm with my aunt, my three sisters and brother and we would go across to the farm to get our milk. My aunt was a great friend of Miss Chate and two mornings a week I would be sent to help her do some cleaning. After I had finished Miss Chate would tell me to sit down and she would give me some cake and milk.

Mrs. E. Creighton

Above: Liverpool Street looking north to Albion Hill in 1963, with view of Chate's Farm. These two streets were built in in 1859-1860. Dinapore Street and the west side of Liverpool Street were demolished in 1965.

Opposite: Richmond Farm Dairy at Chate's Farm in 1934. Few people knew about these buildings hidden in the triangle of Albion Hill, Richmond Street and Liverpool Street. They were approached by a narrow lane from 116 Albion Hill. Chate's Farm was established in the 1860s and the cows were grazed on land across Albion Hill where Grove Street is now. This street was not built until 1894, many years later than the neighbouring streets. The cows were then taken to graze on Tarner's land off Richmond Street, which in turn was built on in 1930. The Chate family lived in 34 Richmond Street with stables and cow stalls ajoining. Delivery of milk ceased during the First World War but customers were still served at the premises until about 1934.

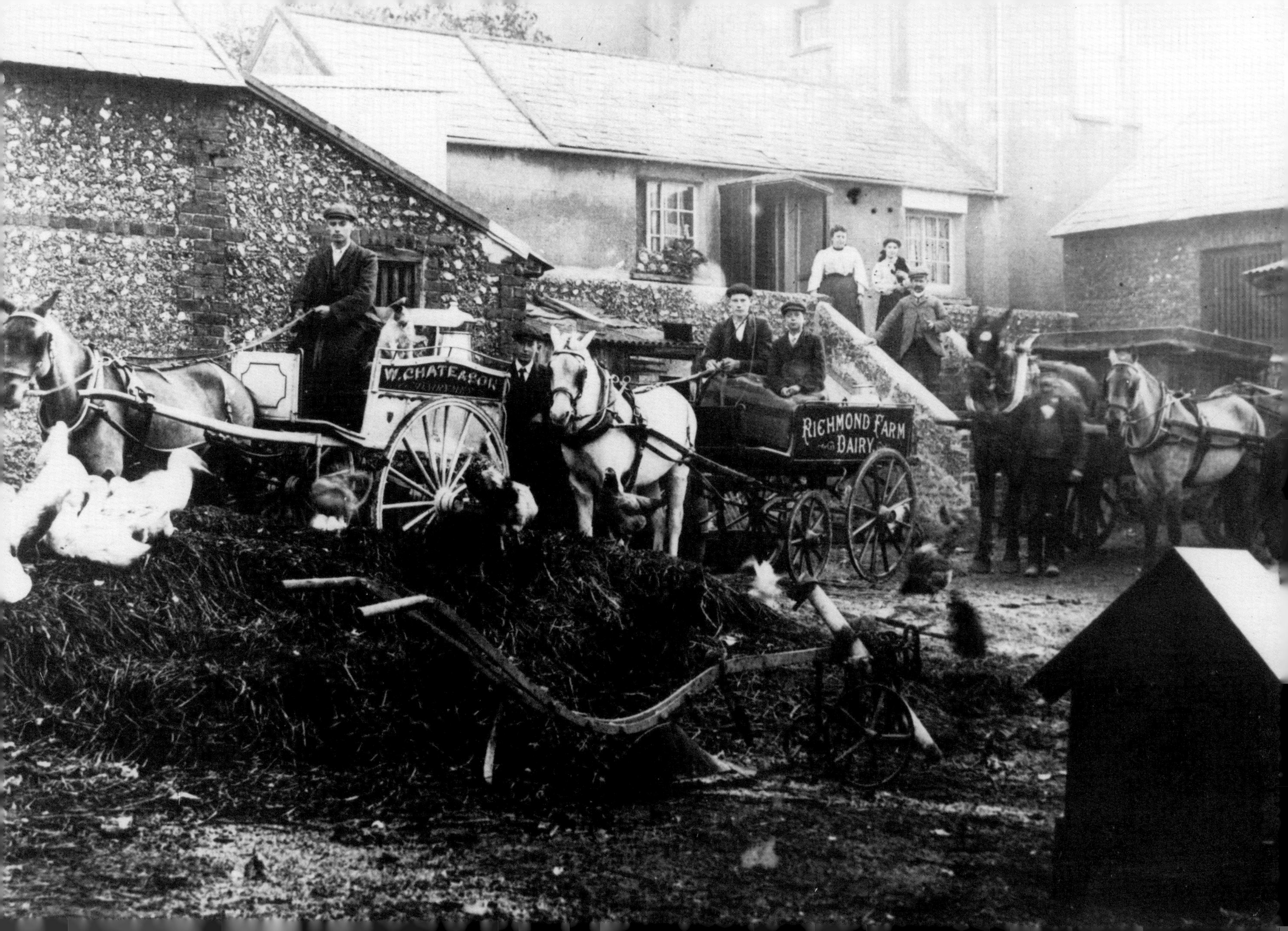

W. CHATE & SON
RICHMOND FARM
DAIRY

50 Southampton Street Abstract of Title 15th June 1869, later the site of the pickle factory

"A conveyance between Thomas Wisden of the first part, Charles Chalk on the second part and Seth Chatterton of Brighton, builder for four plots of a garden site on the North East side of a new street called Southampton Street. Two pauls late Seagers and six pauls formerly Thomas Friends, of 64 foot long by 52 foot wide, abutting on the N.W. side to a messe belonging to Edwin Marwick, on the S.E. side to ground belonging to the said Charles Chalk, on the N.E. to land then or late belonging to Mr. Fieldus and on the S.W. to the road or street called Southampton Street.

21st June 1856: Covenant by said S Chatterton, his heirs with said C Chalk & T Wisden . . . that no noisy, noisome, noxious or offensive trade or business should at any time (thereafter) be carried on or permitted in or upon the said habitations at premises thereby conveyed or any part there nor should anything be done or permitted in or upon the said houses which would be a nuisance or annoyance to the owners or occupiers for the time being of the adjoining land then or late of the said C Chalk ...

Three houses were built on land 48'x 52' nos 49, 50 & 51 Southampton Street. In December 1887 Mr George Edward Mills, a coal dealer of 22 Marlborough Street bought number 50 and in 1906 bought a parcel of land situate in the rear of premises fronting on Finsbury Road and a 10' roadway leading into Islingword Road on the North by an old shed and the premises lastly above described on the West by property belonging to William Smith on the East by property belonging to Reverend W Dinnick together with the stables, outhouses and premises thereon erected . . .

Steps were built in the back garden of number 50 Southampton Street which provided access to the yard which stables the horses and carts used in the delivery of coal. The land then contained 12 stables, 4 store sheds, 1 large cart shed and a large yard. The rear wall of the garden still shows the signs of the steps although they have been blocked in.

Drains were then required from the yard and the house to be connected to the public sewer which had to be 'cleansed, maintained, amended and repaired by the Convenantors . . . indemnify the Corporation at all times hereafter from and against the costs and expenses of cleansing, maintaining, and repairing the said drains."

In 1870 a mortgage of £700 was taken out by Seth Chatterton with The Liberator Permanent Benefit Building Society at 6% over 12 years to purchase the property. The present owner bought the property in 1972, without the yard, for £6,400. The land at the rear of the house became the site of workshops and small factories like the pickle factory.

I lived at 61 Islingword Road as a boy in the 20s and 30s. The Southdown Pickle Factory was at 93 and 94 Islingword Road and ran along the back of Southampton Street. The entrance was like a garage with big doors that you could drive a van through. They pickled cabbage, onions and gherkins in big jars for the trade, and there was always a strong smell of boiling vinegar. It was run by Mr Plummer who employed three people.

Gordon Harwood

After the war the pickle factory In Islingword Road changed from pickles to beetroot and a firm called Grant Curry took it over. They would have ton after ton of beetroots delivered which had to be put into sheds on the site and covered with straw and canvas, and so much would be taken into the factory each day and cooked in vats with yeast, which I think they got from the Phoenix Brewery. They then feed the yeast to the pigs, poor things.

George Inman

[The site of the pickle factory is now used for workshops]

My family were originally tallow merchants and grocers and two of my ancestors were on the committee for the railway, but later their money seemed to run out. I had two older sisters and we had a room in my grandmother's house at 8 Southampton Street where three generations lived in the same house. In 1940 we moved to 22 Southampton Street and in 1942 to number 52 where we live now. My father kept chickens in the back garden and when they had to be killed I took them along to Dick Simmonds at the Charles Napier. My grandfather used to breed rabbits and sell them at Christmas because people couldn't afford a chicken.

After the Second World War there was an old tinker, Mr. Ensore, who had stables and a shop in Finsbury Road at the south end of the 'bad girl's home'. You went through big gates to the sweet cart in one of the stables. For a farthing you could guess at how many sweets he had in a jar, but I never knew anyone who won. Miss Foote had a shop at 75 Southover Street. She had wire netting all over the counter so we couldn't take anything. At one time there were only local people here but when I go to the pub now I'm sometimes the only local person.

Mr. George Inman.

As a child I lived at 18 Southampton Street,. My father was a painter and decorator and my mother had been on the stage before she married. There were five boys and four girls in the family, so the house was crowded. It had three storeys with two rooms at street level, two rooms upstairs and two rooms downstairs. The living room was downstairs with light from a metal grating in the street. We girls slept four 'topped and tailed' to a bed. My mother would take our Sunday dinner to be baked at Hiders the bakers at 103 Islingword Road and then go to the pub with my father until it was ready. She also took her Christmas cake to Hiders to be baked.

Janet Webb nee Jenner

On Christmas day, my father would take the dinners to be cooked. They were ready to be collected at ''turning out time' at the three local pubs. Hot-cross buns were sold on Good Friday at a ha'penny each or seven buns for three pence. On ordinary mornings, hot rolls were always on sale at the bakehouse door for a ha'penny each. The games we played were: hop-scotch, biff bat, yo-yo, skipping and marbles in the gutter. Wednesday nights were 'picture nights', best seats nine pence. We went in our Austin Seven, either to The Court in New Road, The Gaiety or the Lewes Road Troxy, at the bottom of North Road, or The Grand at the top. We were always home by 10.30 pm as my father, who was a master baker, had to make the dough. There were no machines then and he was up at five every morning.

Eve King

My mother always had to work hard as she brought up her brothers and sisters as her mother had died young. She would get up at 6 am and go to bed at midnight and she'd be working all day. She took in washing as well as doing all the washing for the family. She washed everything by hand in the bath, then put it through the mangle. My father did nothing.

I used to push an old pram round to the pickle factory of an evening and get two quarter hundredweight sacks of pickles and bring them home. My mother and older sister would sit all evening with a big enamel bath peeling onions and putting them in bowls of water to keep cool. My mother would also be called on to assist at births and lay people out when they died . I have woken up to find three kids in my bed if their mother had died in the night. She would give us kids a list and we'd knock every door and collect money for a wreath and any spare would be put in an envelope to help with the funeral. My mum died aged sixty four, just when we were all doing well and we could have made her life so much easier.

Ron Richardson, deceased

I was one of six children and times were hard so as children we earned money where we could. I did gardening and I sometimes had work from Mr Volks who would give me a 1/2d and a lump of cake and occasionally a ticket for the railway. I also scrubbed barrels at Tamplin's for a few extra pennies and the Phillips sisters, who ran a florist shop in Baker Street, sometimes gave me flowers for sweeping the front of their shop.

Albert Pattenden

I started working in Edward Street for Mr Jones who had a shop with a dairy at the back when I was 15. I delivered milk on a hand cart. During the war bombs dropped in White Street and damaged the back of the dairy. When I was older and needed to be paid more. I was replaced by another young boy who would work for lower wages.

I then went to work in Preston, where the milk was bottled in a garage, but in 1941 I joined the Co-op dairy at the bottom of Islingword Road, behind Hanover Crescent. Some of the rounds were made by hand cart and some by horse and cart. The horses were stabled at the rear of Hanover Crescent with the horses for the Co-op bakery. The bottling department was between the lane behind Hanover Crescent and the dairy; on the top floor the milk was pasteurised and on the bottom it was bottled, mostly by women.

After the war we had electric carriers which had batteries in a box and a handle to start and stop, which was a lot easier than pushing the cart all the way to Moulsecoomb and Coldean. There was competition between the dairies and you would try to collect all the bottles you delivered but sometimes other dairies took your bottles. They used to have a collection man who would stop you to check that you didn't have bottles from other dairies. Milk was 8d a pint after the war and households were rationed to three pints a day with 3/4 pint for children. Originally the milk bottles had cardboard tops but in the 1970s the shape of the bottle changed and had foil tops.

At one time the Co-op employed over one hundred staff at Hanover Crescent and they also bought over half the houses there and used them as flats for the milkmen and their families. In 1986 the dairy was taken over by the Portsmouth Co-op and they had a new depot built in Moulsecoomb Way and the Hanover Crescent depot closed. It was the end of an era for the area and for myself as I was retired from work. It had been a hard physical job, especially in bad weather, but I have very fond memories of working there.

Frank Edwards.

Below: Jock Harvey with Joe James in the delivery cart from James' dairy in Richmond Street

My father had a job with the Co-op dairy delivering milk on a hand cart and he was offered the house next door to the depot in Toronto Terrace. It was the largest house in the street and had originally been used as a laundry. All the push barrows were kept at the depot and the milk would be piled three storeys high, with eggs and butter in a little cupboard at the bottom. After the round all the milkmen had to use a hose pipe and scrub their barrows. When my father had finished his round in the Hanover area he had to go to London Terrace to pay in the money. It was a very heavy job because of all the hills and there were quite a few accidents with the hand carts running away. My mother always said it damaged his heart and that was the reason he died young. We left Toronto Terrace after my sister became ill with diphtheria and the doctors advised that the milk running from the carts into our gardens had probably caused it.

Vera Saunders nee Rhodes

On summer evenings in the 1950s people would sit outside their front doors on upright chairs keeping an eye on children playing in the street. If we chalked on the walls we would get a clip on the ears. Gangs of children roamed round their own territory, in icy weather we would slide down Albion Hill on tin trays. Totters with horses sold their wares, winkles and mussels were sold from a barrow on Sundays and an Indian gentleman with a turban and a leather case sold wonderful silks. The 'Onion Johnnies' from France with their bicycles sold strings of onions.

Susan Davies

I lived at 24 Windmill Street during the 20s & 30s. My father worked for the gas company. The house had three bedrooms with green wooden Venetian blinds and a cellar with a trap in the front forecourt so that the coal could be poured down. We saw children standing outside pubs as we walked to church on Sundays.

Mrs. Edna Dray nee Bristow

You could get everything you wanted in Richmond Buildings and it stayed open until the 'devil's dancing hours'. Mrs. Smith on the corner of Hanover Terrace sold everything, if she didn't have it in she'd get it for you.

Mrs. Kathleen Lilley

Dorey's Pawn shop was on the corner of Islingword Road. I remember wearing my best suit for visiting relatives and being told not to get anything down it because it was going back into pawn. We pawned our sheets and blankets when times were hard and slept with our overcoats on.

Mr. Albert Saunders.

It used to be a stable community, our front door was always open. Now there are only three of the older people left in the street, it's mostly students and nobody stops to talk to you. We've had police breaking down a door in a drugs raid. They asked us what we wanted to see in the Community Centre but they have things like the beer festival which is not of any interest to us. Years ago the Church of the Annunciation used to have dances and we enjoyed those.

Charles and Ethel Moore (Jim and Goo)

My mother's grandparents (Sebastian Indeman Brazier) lived at 5 Lewes Street in the early 20s. All families lived near each other and didn't move away. My mother's parents lived in Grove

Street and had ten children. I can remember their house with gas mantles and a black range and an outside wc with an original Victorian cistern. Everywhere smelt of lavender polish. The living room was for visitors and they kept their nice pieces in there. I never stayed in there for long.

There was no front garden but there was a boot scraper by the front door and the back windows opened onto a small yard. Coal was delivered and put under the stairs. My grandfather bought the house in the 1920s for £250 cash and it was sold after my aunt's death in 1975 for £5,000 and now houses are being sold in Grove Street for over £90,000. I remember Grove Street as friendly and homely, people were always out on the street and knew everybody, I used to love going there.

Roy Wilkinson

My mother bought bars of Sunlight soap, Monkey Brand bars and square white pumice stone like blocks, which when dipped in cold water and rubbed on the front steps, used to dry to a dazzling white. It took some time to dry, so mum used to either have a little chat to the neighbours, or else polish the red tiles on the courtyard with Red Cardinal polish.

The Quebec laundry was in Quebec Street where there was always a lovely fresh soapy smell; all the sheets were hung out to dry along the back of the gardens of Quebec Street and Montreal Road. I don't know what happened if it rained, but at the end of the week the clean sheets were delivered back, starched and dazzling white, neatly tied in brown paper parcels.

Goldsmith and Towner the bakers in Toronto Terrace was a lovely place; it was a wholesale bakery, but one could always go round and buy rolls from the men in the mornings. I did wonder if perhaps this was a way of putting a few more pennies in their pockets! The aroma was gorgeous, it was a lovely 'smelly' area to live in in those days.

Of course the big thick iron railing that stretched along the road near the bottom of Albion Hill, that was to stop the baker's vans and the milk barrows from sliding down to the bottom in the bad weather. We kids thought it was for our enjoyment to jump and swing on.

Mrs. June Marshall nee Pearce,

My mother, now 100 years old, was the youngest daughter of nine children and lived with her parents at 46 Coleman Street - where my brother and I grew up. Her family had been very poor when she was young and she walked with my Uncle Harry to Dyke Road to the nuns to get food. I used to go to Cartwrights in New Road every week to pay the twelve shillings rent.

The Horse and Groom was on the corner of Coleman Street and Dad liked a drink. The children would hang about the bottle and jug department and if we were lucky we would be given an arrowroot biscuit, Smith's crisps with the salt in blue paper and a lemonade.

When trolley buses first came into use we all had a free ride around the Level. When they took up the tram lines with wooden block, we would buy or pinch the wood for the fire. My grandfather chopped up the blocks but they had flint in them and when they heated you heard a 'ping' and the flint would shoot out.

We used to go to the Arcadia cinema, known as 'The Scratch' in Lewes Road where the Labour Club is now. Bert the dustman was the 'chucker outer' if you were noisy, and they would come round and spray 'flit spray' which smelt foul.

Patrick Cheeseman

Richmond Street c1914. The Richmond public house on the left before it was modernised, below Moodie's fish shop and Peacock's furniture dealers. At the bottom right the Flyman's Home public house is on the corner of Sussex Place. The turret of Richmond Street school can be seen. Note the wall across the top of the street to stop the horses and carts from slipping down.

RICHMOND STREET, HERBERT STREET

Dolly Rogers had a pease pudding and faggot shop in Islingword Road and she gave piano lessons upstairs. During the war we only went to school for half days as there were evacuees. Some of the children who came were very poor and the Brighton families had to clothe them. When their mothers came to see them they all sat in the gutters and talked to each other.

Mrs. Margaret Miller.

I was born in Carlyle Street, the fourth of seven children although the youngest child of my own father. My father was killed in the 1914-18 war and my mother remarried and had three more children. She went out nursing the Indian troops at the Pavilion and the younger children were looked after by my mother's brothers and sisters. She rode everywhere on her bike in order to work.

There was a lot of unemployment in the 20s & 30s but my stepfather was a worker and would turn his hand to anything, but even he was unemployed at times. People would say that if he was out of work then there was no work to be had.

We had a bath in a half barrel, the girls on Friday night and the boys on Saturday. When I was thirteen I was allowed to go to Cobden Road Baths which cost 4d. A number was given to you as you sat in a waiting room while the bath was cleaned.

There were cornfields to the left of Queen's Park Road and beside Queen's Park Pub was Chalky Lane, now Pankhurst Avenue, but there were allotments and Humphrey's farm. The council houses were built in the 1920s.

Elm Grove was built with wooden blocks and the trams went up to the top and along Queen's Park Road from the railway works. At dinner time the trams would run from New England Road and didn't stop, so the men had to jump off and on.

Elm Grove on race days was a terrific mixture of classes, and the inmates of the workhouse were allowed to put their begging bowls or hats over the wall. I didn't think of it much when I was a kid but it was tragic really putting out caps on string. Times were hard but the streets were safe and as children we went all over the place.

Jack Smith

When my father married in 1919 he bought 10 Washington Street for £250. From 1905-1912 the house had been joined to number 9 next door and used as the Annunciation Mission House where the Sisters of Bethany, who did a lot of good work lived there. They were transferred to a house in Hanover Crescent and the Church of the Annunciation sold the houses. The church attracted people from outside the area and they would arrive in their horse and traps, their families having long connections with the church.

Number 8 Washington Street was a sort of off licence or beer shop where you went into their front room and they kept the barrels at the back. On the corner of Jackson Street there was Harley's the grocer who had a manhole in the middle of his floor and he used to go down it to get to his basement.

On Good Friday when I was small, my dad would bring a scaffold rope home and all the children would come and skip in the street. The area was more friendly when I was young, if one was in trouble all were in trouble, and they would give you their last crust of bread. Now a lot of people don't speak to each other. There are only three of the original families left in the street.

Betty Bergin

Above: 'Clydesdale' formerly North Lodge, 10 Richmond Terrace c1905. Built c1849, the earliest conveyance, including a plan, describes it as a large house and coach house lately built for Amon Henry Wilds in the 5th furlong of Hilly Laine. It remained a private house until 1898 when it became the Northern Branch of the Lying-In Institute. The only maternity hospital in Sussex, it was funded by subscribers, who were entitled to recommend patients. It provided lying-in wards for normal deliveries, hospital wards for difficult births and other gynaecological cases, as well as a dispensary for out-patients, and a domiciliary midwifery service. It was bought from R M Welsford by Brighton Corporation in 1895, demolished and the site became part of the site of the Municipal Technical School.

Overleaf: 12 Richmond Terrace

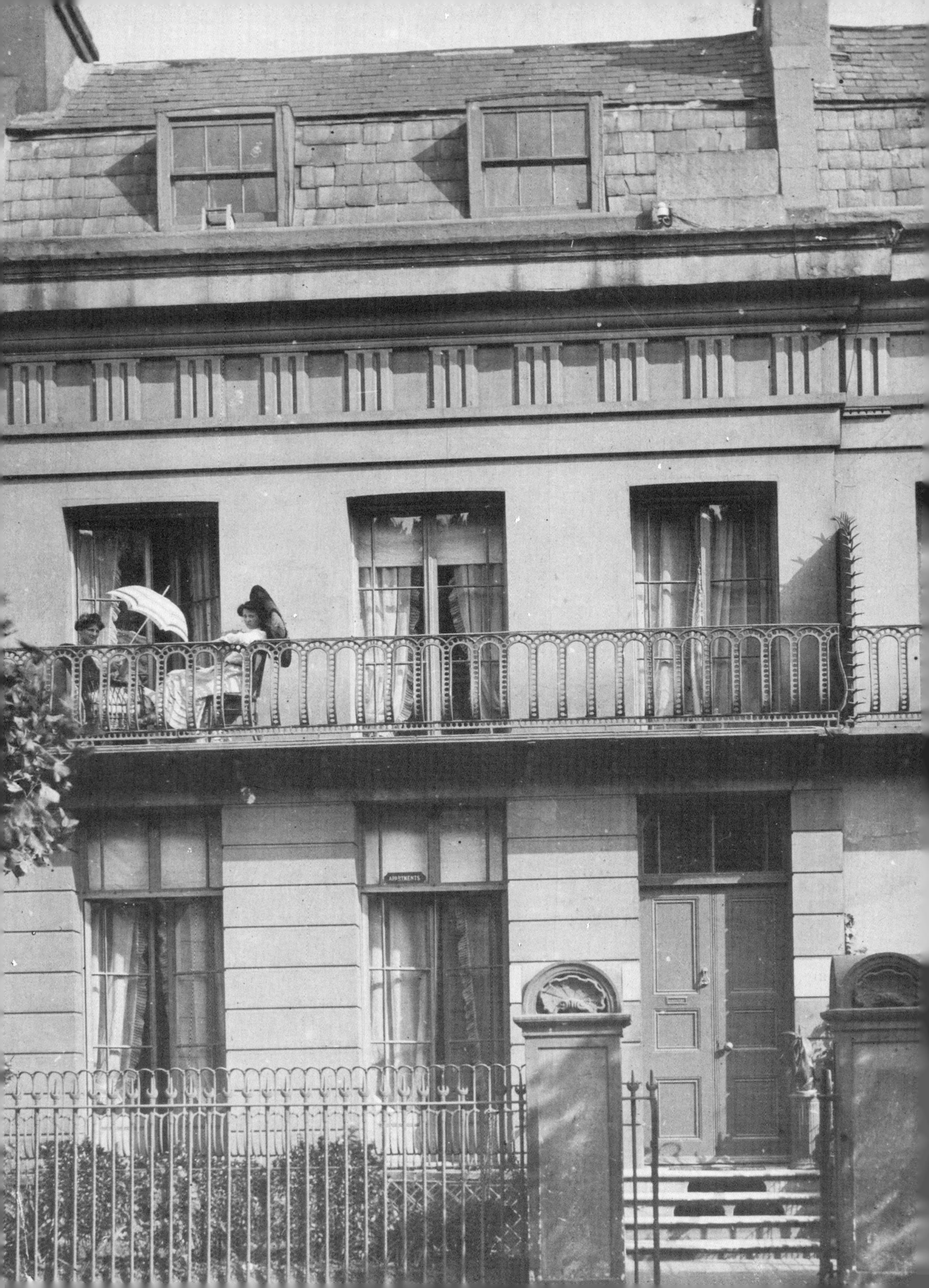
APARTMENTS

Shops

Archer's 128 Islingword Road *Above: J C Archer with his 'boy', Stuart Johnson, who lived in Richmond Buildings. He left school at 14 and worked full time for J C Archer who taught him as much as he could in spite of the shortage of meat. In 1946 he left to do his National Service.*

My grandfather Jesse Archer moved to Brighton to open the Sainsbury's shop in St. James's Street; he planned to build up the trade and open his own shop, hoping to take some of the trade. He leased a shop in Richmond Buildings and many of his customers came with him. He wore a blue serge long dress coat with white cuffs, and later he wore a white coat, apron, shirt sleeves and a straw hat, or a white coat and a trilby. In the 1930s there was no refrigeration, so ice boxes were used, the ice being delivered every two weeks. During the war my grandfather sheltered in the ice box during air raids. He would sometimes leave his shop unattended while he went for a drink in The Lennox Arms opposite, but his customers always knew where he was and called in at the pub to ask to be served. His customers were loyal to him and he treated them well. During the war when the men came home on leave he would allow the women extra rations.

After the war Richmond Buildings became part of a Slum Clearance Area and one by one the shops closed. My grandfather was one of the last to leave as he refused the shop they offered him in Richmond Parade, as he felt the community would take time to build up again. He finally moved to 128 Islingword Road where the shop is today. My grandfather died soon afterwards.

From the age of eight I helped in the shop, skinning rabbits and turning the sausage machine. Sometimes I went to the meat market in Russell Street to help select the meat which was delivered by carrier. In the 1960s there were twelve butchers in the area, but with the growth of the supermarkets small shops closed. The BSE scare caused trade to drop even more and we decided to deal only in organic meat and buy directly from farms. This has improved our trade and more people are turning away from the supermarkets and rediscovering the small butcher.

Brian Archer

128 ISLINGWORD ROAD, BRIGHTON.

Aug 27   190*

M Rusbridger

Bot. of EDWARD GEORGE, BUTCHER.

The Cook Shop, 135 Islingword Road

My great grandmother Frances Ladd (1850 -1936) opened a cook shop at 135 Islingword Road. She had twenty two live births in twenty three years but only eleven children survived and they all helped with the business as they grew older, especially the girls. They went to the slaughterhouse and bought the offal, only sheep and cow's heads, and boned them for the brains, tongue and flesh on the cheek. The meat pies were made with scraps and kidneys and the cooking was done in big ovens housed in the backyard. New potatoes would be swilled around in a barrel with a besom broom because they were easier to peel than old potatoes. They grew their own sage and onion for the pies in their own greenhouses. The family would not eat their own produce but would buy joints of beef from Mr. Warner, the butchers next door.

The shop was successful and Frances bought 11 Islingword Road and the coal yard opposite with the profits. They kept the barrow used for collecting the meat in the coal yard and employed a boy, called Tom whatever his name, usually big for his age, to come straight from school and assist them with the heavier work. They started to bag the coal up in small bags and sell it at the cook shop, this was popular because there was just enough coal in each bag for one night. Later my grandmother Edith Sully and her husband took over the cookshop.

Mrs. Sonia Waterton nee Sully

Benjamin and Frances Ladd on the occasion of their silver wedding at Islingword Place c1895

F J Harman greengrocers, 137 Islingword Road.

My father owned the greengrocer's at 137 Islingword Road for over forty years. He went to the market at Black Lion Street every Tuesday and Saturday and opened seven days a week, Sunday until after lunch. He closed weekdays at about 6 pm but if there was trade still about he would stay open. He bought some of his produce from Henfield, and Worthing tomatoes graded with different coloured paper. He sold firewood and coal and did some removals too.

Arthur Harman

Rackham's grocery shop, 32 Richmond Buildings.

We moved to Brighton in the early 1930s and my stepfather rented a grocery shop at 32 Richmond Buildings for 30 shillings per week, and we lived above it. There were other grocers in the street and he didn't really make a good living. My stepfather felt that he had been misled as to the trade he might expect. The shop was open from 7.30 am-6 pm every day except Sunday when we closed at 1 pm. We weren't allowed to sell groceries on a Sunday, only cigarettes and firewood.

The shop was opposite the 'Lennox Arms' and on Friday and Saturday night when I went up to the cold attic to bed with just a candle for light, I would enjoy the piano playing and singing coming from the bar. During the war it was my job to cut out all the coupons, count them and send them to the Ministry of Food as my stepfather didn't like doing this as it was so fiddley.

John Rackham

Memories of 102 Richmond Street, Brighton

In 1952 we were looking for a small grocery shop and found 102 Richmond Street at a reasonable rent. Brighton Council informed us by letter that no development plan for the area was likely in the next twenty years. We moved in during 1952, but imagine our dismay when in 1953 Brighton Council published a plan for redevelopment of the area of our shop. I think it was probably two years before the clearance started, but after that we saw surrounding houses knocked down with nothing to replace them. We knew one family with two young children who had bought their little terraced house with a mortgage, and spent a lot of money improving it, who were given £5 for their property, which was what most people received. We were more fortunate as the new lease, the letter and the low rent enabled us to claim all we had spent on the property. Gradually all our customers were moved to areas on the edge of the town.

When we first arrived food was still rationed and we had several new customers who registered with us. I think the butter and cheese rations were only 2 oz per person per week. Biscuits were weighed into bags from large tins with glass lids and sliced bread had just started.

Our main wholesalers were Button's in Cheltenham Place and Gravett's at the bottom of Trafalgar Street. Gravett's sold mostly tinned foods, but Button's sold bacon and a wide range of foods. At one time they offered us some 10lb tins of German ham and as we had just bought a slicer we decided to try it. This was a great success and people came from all over the place just for the ham. At Christmas time people would order bacon joints and we would buy sides of bacon which we cut up to order. We sold cigarettes and we split the packets and let people have one or two at a time as this was all they could afford. We didn't have much trouble with bad debts although we did have a 'book', but people mainly settled every week, which we tried to insist on.

We had no refrigerator but the cellar stayed the same temperature all year round. One very hot summer we had to keep our butter there, which we weighed out in two and four ounce packs, this meant we had to go up and down stairs, so we bought a cool box, an OsoCool, but it grew mould inside. We also sold bundles of chopped firewood. We weighed dried fruit, split peas, lentils, rice etc. and older people will remember the blue paper which came in squares, which the grocer had to fold into a cone shape, called a 'poke', and tuck in the top.

Mrs. Betty Parsons

Butcher's Shop 83 Southover Street, Brighton.

My father William Cheesman started working in the shop when he was twenty years old. I think it had always been a butcher's shop and they originally slaughtered the animals at the rear. From the age of twelve I helped my father, mostly with deliveries, because people didn't have refrigerators then and liked to have their meat fresh on Saturdays, when my father worked from 6 am-5 pm.

The meat came from the Russell Street abattoir but later it transferred to Hollingdean Road. We went on Mondays to select meat and anything big was delivered, but if we needed something urgently we would go any day. My father would stay up all night for two or three days before Christmas trussing the birds and, as there was no refrigeration, it was hoped that they would all sell. On Christmas day my father would be ill as a result.

After the Second World War trade was good in the Southover Street area, we had very loyal customers who could buy everything they wanted in the street. At that time there were three butcher's, three boot repairer's, three barber's, three newsagent's, one laundry, four greengrocer's, two chemist's - Mr. O'Flinn had one at the top of the street and his wife had one at the bottom - and six or seven grocer's who also sold hardware. There were many pubs on street corners and along the adjoining streets. Trade began to change about twenty years ago with the development of the supermarkets. For ten years trade didn't go down but didn't improve, but during the last ten years trade has gone down. My mother still lived above the shop and was burgled one night and all the meat was stolen, so we decided to sell. The shop is now being converted into a house as many other shops in the area have been.

Michael Cheesman.

The Lennox Arms was near our shop and there would often be plenty of 'goings on', the odd fight etc. I would watch from the upstairs window.

Mrs. Barbara Seale

I remember Boniface's on the corner of Jackson Street where we could buy sweets, and Harling's the grocer on the other corner, who sold butter and cheese and had mice in the window.

Mr Albert Moore & Mrs Ethel (Goo) Moore,

The Misses Carter had a sweet shop in Albion Hill where you could buy ice cream or a cone of jelly for a ha'penny. They made all their own toffee and in late summer they would pick the apples from the tree in the back garden for toffee apples. When there were no apples left they would twist the toffee around a stick. They would also melt bars of chocolate and put peanuts in it and call them 'nut brittles'. Unfortunately the shop was bombed during the war and never reopened.

Mrs Jackie Griffiths

Ada Wood had a sweet shop opposite Grove Street which sold sweets and odds and ends, there were mice running all over the stock in the window. At 15 Southover Street there was an old bootmaker, Mr Wood, who would always be in his window, with nails in his mouth as he worked. My gran would go to Goldsmith's the baker in Toronto Terrace to cook her Sunday dinner and at Christmas she took the Christmas cake to be baked there.

Mr Roy Wilkinson

Opposite: C Biddleston 4 Islingword Road, hardware shop 1934-5

C. BIDDLESDEN

Miss Foote lived with her elderly mother at 75 Southover Street, and ran a toy shop. We only remember the little toys, evil tin pea-shooters that cut your lips to ribbons and nearly choked you if you breathed in the dried peas instead of blowing; penny whistles, yo-yos, hoops, matchboxes with surprises such as tiny metal puzzles, the smallest wooden or china dolls, tiny jig-saws, playing cards, biff-bats, mouth organs - which gave out awful noises and cut you to bits. My favourite was a soft ball on elastic covered with stockinette and decorated in red, blue and silver cottons. Miss Foote had another string to her bow, she was a music teacher, and on Saturday mornings held piano and violin lessons. We had no piano at the time so to me it seemed a waste of time, but the resourceful Miss Foote devised a paper keyboard which we had to practise on. Saturday morning was spent in learning scales.

Mrs. June Marshall nee Pearce

I grew up in Grove Street in the 1950s when there was still rationing. Locally we would shop at Tuppen's where you could get the broken bits off the bacon and Hudson's who sold vinegar from barrels. If we went to the big shops in London Road it would be to Woolworth's with their large wooden counters, or Sainsbury's towards Preston Circus where you had to queue at every counter.

Susan Davies

As you entered Haine's the grocer's on the corner of Beaufort Terrace you were engulfed by the smell of Sunlight Soap mixed with that of biscuits and raisins, bacon and cheese.

Janis Ravenett

I lived at Southampton Street and my mother took our Sunday dinner to be baked at Hider's the baker's at 103 Islingword Road and then went to the pub with my father until it was ready. She also took her Christmas cake there to be baked. I remember Foote's toy shop in Southover Street, an ordinary house where she sold toys and sweets in the front room. I liked the plastic dolls that were ha'penny each and could sit in a doll's house. I was taught to play the piano by Miss Foote.

Mrs. Janet Webb nee Jenner

I was born at 22 Montreal Road. My mother always shopped locally, she went to Southwell's - a butcher in Southover Street. I would be sent with a list of the meat for the week and it was delivered by a boy on a bike. Mum always insisted on one and a half pounds of the 10d steak, rather than the 8d per pound because they threw in a kidney. We belonged to the Christmas club there where we saved all year for a big piece of pork, never chicken - we didn't know what chicken tasted like. Mr West the grocer, on the corner of Albion Hill and Montreal Road, sold most things and you could weigh out your own sugar and tea and watch butter being patted out. Mr Collins from Quebec Street came round with his greengrocery barrow, but it was only a front because he took bets. The fishermen also came round selling from their barrows.

The draper's shop in Montreal Road became a launderette and the baker's shop at the bottom of the road has become an estate agent. I loved walking by Puttock's the baker's shop on the way to and from school because of the lovely smell of bread. You could buy yesterday's bread and cakes cheaply, most of us went home for lunch so I would sometimes buy myself a cheap cake.

Miss Olive Denman, deceased. [She lived at 22 Montreal Road.until the end of her life.]

Opposite: 108/109 May's General Stores, Southover Street on the corner of Newhaven Street in 1905. The building has now been converted to flats.

109

LYONS TEA

TETLEY'S TEAS

CLARK'S BREAD

I was born in Montreal Road in 1926. There were a lot of small shops in Islingword Road. The pawnbrokers at 43 Islingword Street was run by Mr. Dorey. My mother, who loved a bargain, bought quite a lot of good class things there, including a canteen of cutlery. My uncle had a butcher's shop at 123 Islingword Road which has recently been made into a house.

Mrs. E. Campbell nee Boyett

I grew up in Hanover Terrace and attended Hanover Terrace school. Before I went to school in the winter I used to go to Measors at 114 Islingword Road. It was a fruiterers but they also sold coal. I used to get a 28lb bag of coal on a trolley and wheel it down Southover Street so that we would have coal for the day. I had to return the trolley before I went to school.

On Saturday night there used to be a market on the Level, which was under canvas and had flares for lighting. My mother would send me down with seven shillings and tell me to wait until a bone of beef got to this price. After 9 pm the traders started to auction their meat and I waited until I heard seven shillings and bought the meat. It used to be enormous and I had difficulty carrying it up Southover Street.

Mrs. Dorothy Farrell nee Page, deceased.

I lived at 24 Windmill Street during the 20s and 30s. My mother shopped locally but also used St James's Street because it was cheaper and you could buy broken biscuits and dried peas that were already soaked. On the corner of Montreal Road there was a baker's and every Saturday afternoon my mother would make a large cake and take it to be baked for six pence.

Mrs. Edna Dray nee Bristow.

Eve King moved to Brighton in the 1920s when she was six years old and lived most of her life at 17 Southover Street. Eve's father was a master baker with a shop on the corner of Coleman Street. At the lower end of Southover Street was a row of small cottages with a touch of countryside. On entering a huge oak door it was like walking into fairytale - a long a garden path flanked with flowers, shrubs, trees and greenhouses. At the end of the path was a lovely farmhouse where you could get butter, eggs and jams and everything smelled delicious.

Payne's milk and greengroceries were delivered by horse and cart. The horse would mount the pavement and come to our shop door for bits. Southover Street was always a dangerous hill, and many times horse carts and lorries delivering beer lost control. I remember that Clarke's Brewery had a horse and cart, and the driver would turn out of Belgrave Street down into Coleman Street; the poor horse would be terrified. One day the cart, driver and horse slithered down the hill and crashed into a lamp post at the corner of Hanover Terrace. A traction engine which delivered flour to our side bakehouse door, also came to the same fate. His brakes failed and the traction engine ended up in the wall of the laundry at the corner of Hanover Street.

Eve King writing in the Hanover Herald

I was born above my parent's shop, which sold groceries and milk, at 94 Richmond Street on the corner of Claremont Row. I was the sixth of eight children, five boys and three girls and my mother stopped working in the shop after I was born. When my father became ill he sold many of the rounds off to the men who worked for him

Mrs. Connie Dowds nee James

Opposite: Lily and Florence Long standing outside their shop in Elm Grove c1905. Their parents Charles and Alice Long can be seen looking through the window

237 ELM GROVE
L&F LONG
CHINA STORES
237
STRAWBERRY
RASPBERRY
PINEAPPLE
PEPPERMINT
CLOVES

RICHMOND STREET, STEEPEST HILL IN BRIGHTON

THE RICHMOND HOTEL

ABBEY & SONS' ENTIRE

RICHMOND PLACE

WARD
STATIONERY
& TOBACCO
PICTURE POST CARDS

SPARE MOMENTS
32233 IN ADVANCE FREE TO ALL 32233

DAILY EXPRESS
STANDARD
EVENING
STANDARD
ST JAMES'S
GAZETTE

HAYS

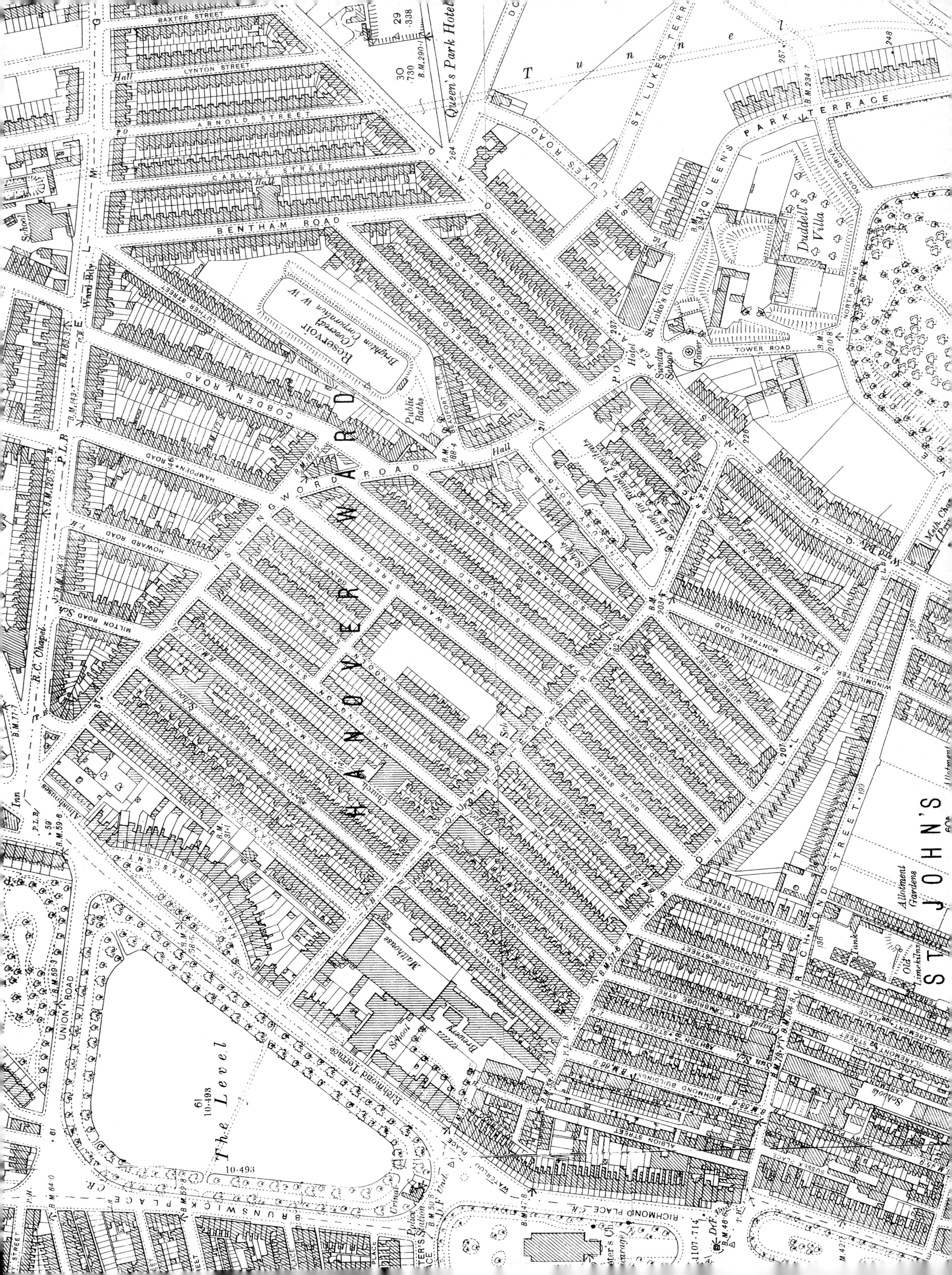

BAXTER STREET
LYNTON STREET
ARNOLD STREET
CARLYLE STREET
BENTHAM ROAD
Hall
School
Queen's Park Hotel
ST. LUKES TERR.
ST. LUKES ROAD
QUEENS PARK TERRACE
QUEENS PARK
Duddell's Villa
NORTH DRIVE
TOWER ROAD
Tower
St. Luke's Ch.
Sunday School
Hotel
Reservoir (Covered)
Brighton Corporation W.W.
LUTHER STREET
COBDEN ROAD
HAMPDEN ROAD
HOWARD ROAD
MILTON ROAD Sch.
R.C. Chapel
Public Baths
BEAUFORT TER.
ISLINGWORD PLACE
ISLINGWORD ROAD
HANOVER WARD
SOUTHAMPTON STREET
ISLINGWORD STREET
EWART STREET
GRANT STREET
WASHINGTON STREET
COLEMAN STREET
HANOVER TERRACE
HANOVER CRESCENT
Almshouses
Inn
Chapel
TORONTO TERRACE
MONTREAL ROAD
QUEBEC STREET
SCOTLAND STREET
HOLLAND STREET
GROVE STREET
JERSEY STREET
NEWARK PLACE
BELGRAVE STREET
LEWES STREET
WINDMILL TER.
LIVERPOOL STREET
RICHMOND STREET
DINAPORE STREET
CAMBRIDGE STREET
ASHTON STREET
RICHMOND BUILDINGS
ALBION STREET
CLAREMONT PLACE
CLAREMONT STREET
SUSSEX PLACE
Schools
Allotment Gardens
ST. JOHN'S
Malthouse
Brewery
School
Richmond Terrace
UNION ROAD
The Level
BRUNSWICK PLACE
WATERLOO PLACE
RICHMOND PLACE
Police Station

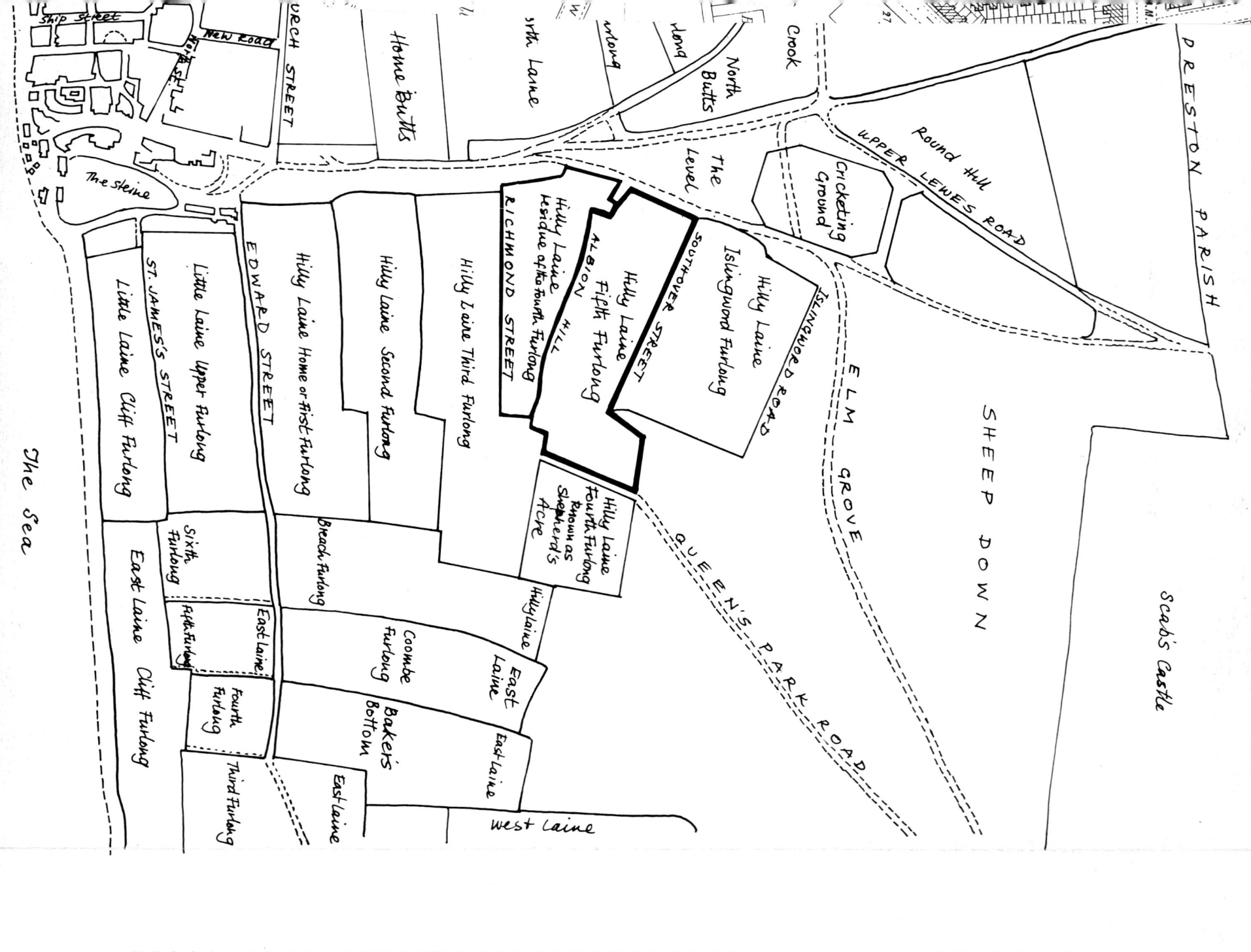

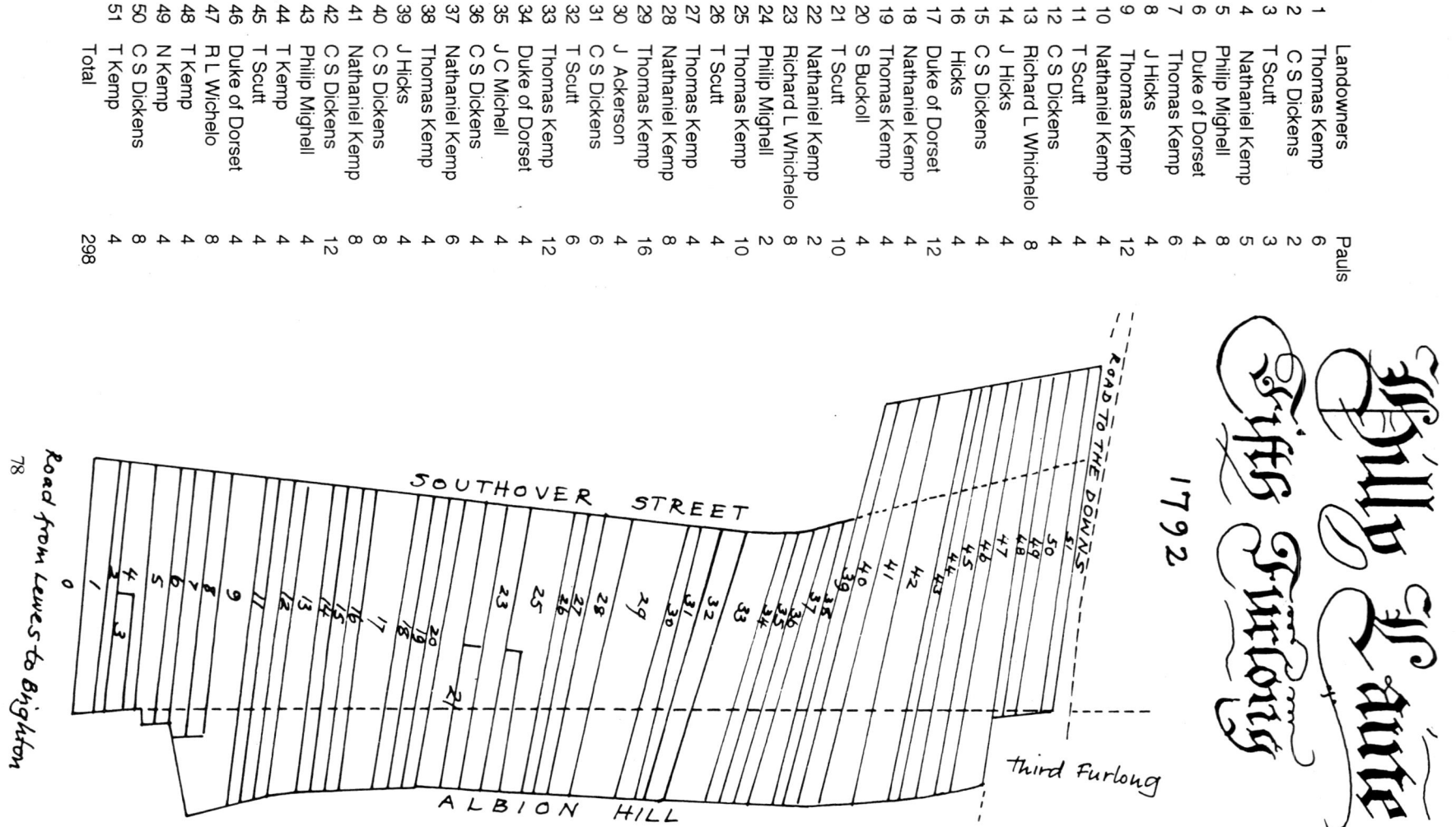

	Landowners	Pauls
1	Thomas Kemp	6
2	C S Dickens	2
3	T Scutt	4
4	Nathaniel Kemp	5
5	Philip Mighell	8
6	Duke of Dorset	4
7	Thomas Kemp	6
8	J Hicks	4
9	Thomas Kemp	12
10	Nathaniel Kemp	4
11	T Scutt	4
12	C S Dickens	4
13	Richard L Whichelo	4
14	J Hicks	4
15	C S Dickens	4
16	Hicks	4
17	Duke of Dorset	12
18	Nathaniel Kemp	2
19	Thomas Kemp	4
20	S Buckoll	4
21	T Scutt	10
22	Nathaniel Kemp	2
23	Richard L Whichelo	8
24	Philip Mighell	2
25	Thomas Kemp	10
26	T Scutt	4
27	Thomas Kemp	8
28	Nathaniel Kemp	8
29	Thomas Kemp	16
30	J Ackerson	4
31	C S Dickens	6
32	T Scutt	6
33	Thomas Kemp	12
34	Duke of Dorset	4
35	J C Michell	4
36	C S Dickens	4
37	Nathaniel Kemp	6
38	Thomas Kemp	4
39	J Hicks	4
40	C S Dickens	8
41	Nathaniel Kemp	8
42	C S Dickens	12
43	Philip Mighell	4
44	T Kemp	4
45	T Scutt	4
46	Duke of Dorset	4
47	R L Wichelo	8
48	T Kemp	8
49	N Kemp	4
50	C S Dickens	8
51	T Kemp	4
Total		298

Hilly Lane Fifth Furlong 1792